BE STILL, MY SOUL

OTHER CROSSWAY BOOKS BY
NANCY GUTHRIE

Come, Thou Long-Expected Jesus
Experiencing the Peace and Promise of Christmas

Jesus, Keep Me Near the Cross
Experiencing the Passion and Power of Easter

BE STILL, MY SOUL

Embracing God's Purpose & Provision in Suffering

*25 Classic & Contemporary Readings
on the Problem of Pain*

Edited by
NANCY GUTHRIE

:: CROSSWAY

WHEATON, ILLINOIS

Be Still, My Soul: Embracing God's Purpose and Provision in Suffering

Copyright © 2010 by Nancy Guthrie

Published by Crossway
      1300 Crescent Street
      Wheaton, Illinois 60187

Cover design: Amy Bristow

Cover photo: Michael Trevillion, Trevillion Images

First printing 2010

Printed in the United States of America

Chapter opening quotations, the preface, and chapter 3 Scripture quotations are from the ESV® Bible (*The Holy Bible, English Standard Version*®), copyright © 2001 by Crossway Bibles, a publishing ministry of Good News Publishers. Used by permission. All rights reserved.

Chapters 1, 11, 16, 19, and 21 Scripture references are from *The Holy Bible: New International Version.*® Copyright © 1973, 1978, 1984 by International Bible Society. Used by permission of Zondervan Publishing House. All rights reserved.

The "NIV" and "New International Version" trademarks are registered in the United States Patent and Trademark Office by International Bible Society. Use of either trademark requires the permission of International Bible Society.

Chapter 5 Scripture references are from *The New King James Version.* Copyright © 1982, Thomas Nelson, Inc. Used by permission.

Chapters 7, 9, and 25 Scripture quotations are from the *King James Version* of the Bible.

Chapter 8 Scripture references are from *The New Revised Standard Version.* Copyright © 1989 by the Division of Christian Education of the National Council of the Churches of Christ in the U.S.A. Published by Thomas Nelson, Inc. Used by permission of the National Council of the Churches of Christ in the U.S.A.

Chapters 20 and 22 Scripture references are from *The Revised Standard Version.* Copyright © 1946, 1952, 1971, 1973 by the Division of Christian Education of the National Council of the Churches of Christ in the U.S.A.

Scripture references marked PHILLIPS are from *The New Testament in Modern English*, translated by J. B. Phillips © 1972 by J. B. Phillips. Published by Macmillan.

All emphases in Scripture quotations have been added by the author.

Trade paperback ISBN: 978-1-4335-1185-1
PDF ISBN: 978-1-4335-1186-8
Mobipocket ISBN: 978-1-4335-1187-5

Library of Congress Cataloging-in-Publication Data

   Be still, my soul : embracing God's purpose and provision in suffering : 25 classic and contemporary readings on the problem of pain / Nancy Guthrie, editor.
      p. cm.
   Includes index.
   ISBN 978-1-4335-1185-1 (tpb)
   1. Suffering—Religious aspects—Christianity. 2. Consolation.
I. Guthrie, Nancy. II. Title.
BV4909.B4   2010
248.8'6—dc22   2009031456

Crossway is a publishing ministry of Good News Publishers.

VP		20	19	18	17	16	15	14	13	12	11
14	13	12	11	10	9	8	7	6	5	4	3

I affectionately and admiringly dedicate this book
to my friend,

JONI EARECKSON TADA

Years ago, I stood at the back of a hotel ballroom listening to Joni speak and wondered to myself, "What is it that makes her so compelling? What makes people listen so closely to what she has to say?" And the answer to my question was obvious. It's her suffering. Joni's suffering gives her credibility to speak. We listen because she lives where only our deepest fears take us. And we listen because the way she articulates how she has made sense of her suffering helps us to make sense of ours.

Years later, when I met Joni, I told her that I hoped that I would be as good a steward of my suffering as she has been of hers. But I fear that is too lofty an aim, too high a hurdle. Joni not only shows me, and the rest of the world, how to persevere as a faithful steward of suffering, she shows us how to serve out of our suffering and how to radiate joy in the midst of our suffering. Mostly she shows us what it looks like to love Jesus even as she lives day-by-day in the fellowship of sharing in his sufferings.

Let every trial teach me more of thy peace,
more of thy love.

Thy Holy Spirit is given to increase thy graces,
and I cannot preserve or improve them unless he
works continually in me.

May he confirm my trust in thy promised help,
and let me walk humbly in dependence upon thee,
for Jesus' sake.

FROM *THE VALLEY OF VISION*

Contents

Preface   9

Part One
GOD'S PERSPECTIVE ON SUFFERING

1   Suffering: The Servant of Our Joy   15
    Tim Keller

2   The Gift of Pain   23
    Philip Yancey

3   God's Plan A   31
    Joni Eareckson Tada

4   When We Don't Know Why, We Trust God   37
    Who Knows Why
    Os Guinness

5   Is There Such a Thing as Senseless Tragedy?   43
    R. C. Sproul

6   Illumined by the Light of Divine Providence   49
    John Calvin

7   A Profound Answer to the Pressing Question, "Why?"   55
    Wilson Benton Jr.

8   Bearing Suffering   63
    Dietrich Bonhoeffer

9   No Sorrow Like Jesus' Sorrow   69
    John Newton

Part Two
GOD'S PURPOSE IN SUFFERING

10 The God We Had We Lose   75
    Abraham Kuyper

11 When Cost Becomes Privilege   81
    Helen Roseveare

12 Prepared for Usefulness   87
      A. W. Tozer

13 The Test of a Crisis   91
      Martyn Lloyd-Jones

14 Too Good to Suffer?   99
      St. Augustine

15 Faith Tried and Proved   103
      Charles Haddon Spurgeon

16 Choosing Trust   109
      Jerry Bridges

17 Dying Well   113
      D. A. Carson

Part Three
GOD'S PROVISION IN SUFFERING

18 Just What You Need, Just in Time   121
      Corrie ten Boom

19 Dark Valleys   127
      Sinclair Ferguson

20 Hoped-for Healing   135
      J. I. Packer

21 Happy in Affliction   141
      Thomas Manton

22 Power in Weakness   145
      John Piper

23 To Suffer as Christ Did   153
      Martin Luther

24 Learning to Be Content   161
      Jeremiah Burroughs

25 Refuge and Rest in Christ   167
      Jonathan Edwards

Notes   171

Scripture Index   173

Preface

A while ago, a Bradford pear tree in our backyard cracked and split and had to be removed. Seeking to shield our neighbors from the horror of seeing into the inside of our messy garage, we had three evergreen trees planted in its place. But one of them just wouldn't take root and repeatedly fell over. We would prop it up, pressing in the dirt around it, only to find it had blown down again a short time later when a swift wind blew.

Honestly, I had about given up on getting the evergreen to take root and thrive when my parents came to visit. As we pulled into the driveway, we saw that the tree had fallen down again. Even before going into the house, my dad found an old broom handle in the garage and some rope. He plunged the rod deep into the ground by the tree and tethered the tree to it with the rope. From that time on, no matter how hard the wind blew, the tree didn't fall down. Today, it is still standing tall.

Few of us get through life without having the winds of difficulty blow through our lives at some point—cold and unrelenting winds that threaten to knock us down for good. And when the winds of suffering blow in our lives, what we need most is something secure to tether ourselves to, something strong and unmovable that will keep us from being swept away in a storm of questions, fear, discouragement, and disillusionment.

The writer to the Hebrews describes just what we need, just what God has provided to us. "So when God desired to show more convincingly to the heirs of the promise the unchangeable character of his purpose, he guaranteed it with an oath, so that by two unchangeable things, in which it is impossible for God to lie, we who have fled for refuge might have strong encouragement to hold fast to the hope set before us. We have this as a sure and steadfast anchor of the soul . . . " (Heb. 6:17–19).

An "anchor of the soul." That's what we want and need—to have something solid and secure to hold on to so we can live our lives at rest rather than being blown to and fro by every new circumstance that threatens us. The writer to the Hebrews tells us to "hold fast to the hope set before us." In other words, he is telling us to tether ourselves securely to what God has said, to the promises of God. And we know that "all the promises of God find their Yes" in Jesus Christ (2 Cor. 1:20). Jesus himself is God's grand "yes!" to us, the hope set before us to hold on to.

It was when my husband, David, and I had a daughter we named Hope that we were forced, in a sense, to discover what it means to "hold fast to the hope set before us." I'm not sure I even understood what "hope" really meant when we gave her that name. I just liked the sound and simplicity of it. But in the days following her birth, when we discovered that due to a rare metabolic disorder her life would be very short and very difficult, when the situation in human terms seemed hopeless, I began my search for understanding what hope really means, and what it means to hold fast to it.

During Hope's life and following her death, and then again when we had a second child who had the same fatal syndrome as Hope had, David and I reached out to grab hold of the promises of God in the person of Jesus Christ like never before. Suffering does that. It pushes us deeper into the mystery of God. It makes us more desperate for him, to hear from him and sense his presence. We found the solid rock of Scripture was our sure foundation, reshaping our understanding and expectations of God, instilling us with confidence in the character and purposes of God.

Holding on to hope, for us, has not been a vague, sentimental experience. It has been an ongoing choice to believe God's Word. We have sought to understand and embrace God's perspective on suffering and bring him glory through it (John 9:3). We've grabbed hold of his promise that there is purpose and meaning in our suffering because we are his (Rom. 8:28). We've grabbed hold of the sovereignty of God, believing that he "meant it for good" (Gen. 50:20). We have rested in his presence and provision of joy and strength and faith and perseverance—everything we've needed (2 Cor. 12: 9). We have found that in the darkest of times, he has been with us, comforting us (Ps. 23: 4). We "groan inwardly as we wait eagerly" (Rom. 8:23) for that day when God's promises of resurrection and restoration become reality.

Occasionally someone has said to me, "You must be a very strong person."

But I know the truth—that *I am not strong.*

However, I am tethered to Someone who is strong.

I am not holding on to hope in terms of a positive perspective about the future or an innate sense of optimism, but rather holding on to the living person of Jesus Christ. I am grabbing hold of the promises of God, his purposes, and his provision, and refusing to let go.

I suppose that is why collecting this great writing on God's perspective, purpose, and provision in suffering has been such a great joy to me. The scriptural truths elucidated in this book by respected classic and contemporary theologians and Bible teachers are the truths that have been the solid foundation under my feet in the storms of suffering and sorrow in my life.

I pray they will provide that for you as well—that they will shape your thinking, steel your resolve, and still your soul.

Nancy Guthrie

Part One

GOD'S PERSPECTIVE ON SUFFERING

1

Suffering:
The Servant of Our Joy

TIM KELLER

So we do not lose heart. Though our outer self is
wasting away, our inner self is being renewed day by
day. For this light momentary affliction is preparing
for us an eternal weight of glory beyond all comparison.

2 Corinthians 4:16–17

We live in a unique culture. Every other society before ours has been more reconciled to the reality that life is full of sorrow. If you read the journals of people who lived before us, it is obvious they understood this, and that they were never surprised by suffering. We are the first culture to be surprised by suffering. When Paul writes to the people of his day, "We do not lose heart, though outwardly we are wasting away," he speaks of suffering as a given.

Greek scholars will tell you Paul was not just talking about the body as wasting away, but about all of life in this visible world. He was saying that everything in this world is wearing away. Everything is steadily, irreversibly falling apart.

Our bodies are wearing away. Our hearts are like wind-up clocks with a finite number of clicks that are clicking away. Our physical appearance and attractiveness are wearing away, and we can't stop it. Our relationships are wearing away. Get a group of friends around you, and time and circumstance will eventually pull you apart. Our families are wearing away, dying off one at a time. Our skills are wearing away. You can't stay on top of your game forever. Everything is like a wave on the sand. You can't pin it down; it starts to recede from you.

Paul writes about "wasting away" to a group of people who have suggested that he can't be trusted, that God is obviously not with him. One reason Paul can't be trusted, they suggest, is that he has experienced an inordinate number of tragedies and difficulties. And, in fact, Paul makes a list of them in 2 Corinthians 11:24–28:

> Five times I received from the Jews the forty lashes minus one. Three times I was beaten with rods, once I was stoned, three times I was shipwrecked, I spent a night and a day in the open sea, I have been constantly on the move. I have been in danger from rivers, in danger from bandits, in danger from my own countrymen, in danger from Gentiles; in danger in the city, in danger in the country, in danger at sea; and in danger from false brothers. I have labored and toiled and have often gone without sleep; I have known hunger and thirst and have often gone without food; I have been cold and naked. Besides everything else, I face daily the pressure of my concern for all the churches.

The people in Corinth were saying, *How can God be with a man when all that stuff happens to him? Surely when God's with you he protects you. When God is with you, you prosper. I've been traveling the Mediterranean all my life and I've never been shipwrecked, and this guy has been shipwrecked three times?*

It's similar to the thinking Job's friends had about Job's suffering. Job's friends said, *If God is with you, this wouldn't happen. God can't be with you. If he was, he'd protect you.*

And we ask ourselves the same thing, don't we, when one thing after another goes wrong, when we've reached the bottom and find out there's lower to go?

This can't be right, we think. *Either there is no God or God is mad at me. He can't be with me or this wouldn't be happening.*

How does Paul respond to this premise? Paul doesn't just say God is with him. He goes further. He says that the suffering and hardship he has experienced is not a denial of the gospel, but a confirmation of the gospel.

He writes, "We are hard pressed on every side, but not crushed; perplexed, but not in despair; persecuted, but not abandoned; struck down, but not destroyed; we always carry around in our body the death of Jesus, so that the life of Jesus may also be revealed in our body. For we who are alive are always being given over to death for Jesus' sake, so that his life may be revealed in our mortal body. So then, death is at work in us, but life is at work in you" (2 Cor. 4:8–12).

Paul says that the suffering and hardship he
has experienced is not a denial of the gospel,
but a <u>confirmation of the gospel</u>.

Paul is saying that the way of the gospel is death leading to resurrection, weakness resulting in triumphant exaltation. Paul is saying that the way the gospel works in Jesus' life is the way it is working in his life. He's saying that just as Jesus' suffering and death led to greater life, he is finding that the same thing is happening in his life. "My deaths seem to lead to greater life," he's saying.

The suffering he experiences because he is trying to minister lead to greater life in other people's lives, as they hear the gospel and experience spiritual life.

And this doesn't just happen in the lives of people in professional ministry. I know a number of people—doctors and lawyers and the like, who, rather than stepping onto the ladder of professional and financial upward mobility, have decided to serve underserved people. They've given their lives to working with the poor in places off the beaten path. And when a person does that, they fall out of the structure of their profession. They kind of go off the radar, and find they can't advance. But they also find that their career death produces greater life.

When we suffer for doing the right thing, when we choose to live unselfishly, we find that our "death" leads to greater life for those around us.

But it is not only people around us who experience greater life when we suffer. In Romans 5:3–5 Paul says, "We also rejoice in our sufferings, because we know that suffering produces perseverance; perseverance, character; and character, hope. And hope does not disappoint us, because God has poured out his love into our hearts by the Holy Spirit, whom he has given us."

Now what is he saying there? He's saying, "My suffering not only leads to greater life in those *around* me, but *in* me."

It's like what happens to an acorn. Do you know how much power there is in an acorn? An entire huge tree can come out of one small little acorn. And out of that tree can come innumerable other trees. One acorn has the power to fill a continent with wood.

But only if it dies. Only if it "falls to the ground and dies" (John 12:24) is that enormous power released.

Every human soul in the image of God has infinitely more life potential than an acorn. Every soul has the capacity for compassion, beauty, greatness, composure, and character—but it will not be released until there is a death, the death that comes through suffering and trials.

Reynolds Price is a Duke University professor who had spinal cancer and survived, but is now a paraplegic. A young medical student who contracted terminal cancer wrote him, asking, "How can you believe in God with all this suffering?" Reynolds Price wrote a whole book back to him. It's called *Letter to a Man in a Fire*. And in it he said a very bold thing at one point to this young medical student with cancer:

> If you survive this ordeal in working condition, you're almost certain to be a far more valuable medical doctor and person than you'd otherwise have been. Poets more ancient than Aeschylus have hymned the awful paradox that humankind can apparently only advance through suffering; but no one has cut that paradox in deeper letters than Aeschylus—"It is God's law that he who learns must suffer. And even in our sleep, pain that cannot forget falls drop by drop upon the heart, and in our own despite, against our will, comes wisdom to us by the awful grace of God."[1]

Unless a seed falls into the ground and dies, it cannot bear life. Suffering leads to life, but that seed has to fall to the ground.

That may sound nice, but how do we know it will really work? Paul tells us how in verse 14 of 2 Corinthians 4: "because we know that the one who raised the Lord Jesus from the dead will also raise us with Jesus and present us with you in his presence." Because Jesus is raised from the dead, it is the very meaning of history that life comes out of death—that out of devastation comes redemption.

Then Paul gives us an example in his own life—he tells us about his "thorn in the flesh." What was his thorn in the flesh? We don't know. What we do know is that Paul asked God to remove it over and over, and God said "no."

Does that remind you of anyone?

In the garden of Gethsemane, Jesus was not just facing a thorn in his flesh, but the ultimate stake through his heart and soul. He repeatedly asked God to remove it, and God said "no."

What God said to Jesus and to Paul, and what he says to us is, "My power always comes to perfection though weakness. My power can only explode into your life through your weakness."

Paul says that if Jesus can uncomplainingly submit to his infinite suffering and thereby have God's life explode into our lives and into the world, then you and I can submit to our finite suffering uncomplainingly and know the same thing will happen. The death in us will work life in us and in others around us. That's our hope.

Death in us will work life in us and in others around us. That's our hope.

But Paul gives us even more to hope for. He writes, "Though outwardly we are wasting away, yet inwardly we are being renewed day by day. For our light and momentary troubles are achieving for us an eternal glory that far outweighs them all" (2 Cor. 4:16–17).

This is a parallel passage to what he wrote in Romans 8:18: "I consider that our present sufferings are not worth comparing with the glory that will be revealed in us." When we put the two together, we see the astonishing claim Paul is making. He's saying that our suffering will be outweighed by future glory, and that our suffering now is actually "achieving for us" that future glory.

Marilyn McCord Adams, who teaches philosophy at Yale, has done a study of female Christian mystics of the Middle Ages. She has distilled out of their teaching some remarkable teachings about suffering. Adams says that the Stoics said to accept suffering, the Epicureans said to avoid suffering, and the aesthetics and masochists said to embrace suffering. But, she points out, the gospel does not accept, avoid, or embrace suffering; it engulfs suffering.

What does that mean? It all has to do with hope.

If heaven is our hope, then heaven will be compensation for all we've lost. But is our greatest hope just heaven?

Our hope is the new heaven and the new earth. Our future hope is a restoration of the world and the life we've always wanted. And that changes everything in regard to suffering.

Years ago I had a terrible nightmare. In my nightmare, every member of my family was killed in terrible fashion. I woke up at 3 a.m., panting from the nightmare. It was if I had lost my family and awakened to discover I had them back. I wanted to wake them all up and hug them. I loved them before the nightmare, but not like I did after the nightmare.

Here's the point. The joy of finding them wasn't a joy *in spite of* the nightmare but a joy *enhanced by* the nightmare.

Because of the nightmare, my joy was intensified. The nightmare was taken up into the joy of having them back. The nightmare actually punctuated my joy.

If heaven is a compensation for all the stuff we wanted that we never had, that is one thing. But if the new heaven and new earth is our hope—and it is—it will make everything horrible we've experienced nothing but a nightmare. And as a nightmare, it will infinitely, correspondingly increase our future joy and glory in a way it wouldn't have been increased if we'd never suffered.

That is the ultimate defeat of evil. To say that our suffering is an illusion or to say we will be compensated for our suffering is one thing. But to say that the suffering we experience now will one day be a servant of our joy does not just compensate for it, it undoes it.

"Our light and momentary troubles are achieving for us an eternal glory that far outweighs them all." There has never been an understanding of suffering that was more hopeful or encouraging.

But to understand it, you have to "fix your eyes on it." That's a discipline. Think about it until it pulverizes your discouragement. Let the glory of it hit you.

Don't just accept suffering—because God doesn't want it.

Don't just avoid suffering—because God can use it.

Don't just embrace suffering—because it is evil.

The evil that hurts us now will be the eventual servant of our joy and glory eternally.

Instead, enjoy the hope that suffering is going to be engulfed, swallowed up. The evil that hurts us now will be the eventual servant of our joy and glory eternally.

Only because he understood this do we have this amazing statement by Dostoevsky in *The Brothers Karamazov*:

> I have a childlike conviction that the sufferings will be healed and smoothed over, that the whole offensive comedy of human contradictions will disappear like a pitiful mirage, a vile concoction of man's Euclidean mind, feeble and puny as an atom, and that ultimately, at the world's finale, in the moment of eternal harmony, there will occur and be revealed something so precious that it will suffice for all hearts, to allay all indignation, to redeem all human villainy, all bloodshed; it will suffice not only to make forgiveness possible, but also to justify everything that has happened with men.[2]

Adapted from "Christian Hope and Suffering," a sermon by Tim Keller given at Redeemer Presbyterian Church, May 16, 2004. Copyright © by Timothy Keller, 2008. All rights reserved. Used by permission.

Tim Keller is founding pastor of Redeemer Presbyterian Church in New York, New York.

Scripture references are from *The Holy Bible: New International Version.*

2

The Gift of Pain

PHILIP YANCEY

> For I consider that the sufferings of this present time are
> not worth comparing with the glory that is to be revealed
> to us. . . . For we know that the whole creation has been
> groaning together in the pains of childbirth until now.
>
> *Romans 8:18, 22*

I have never read a poem extolling the virtues of pain, nor seen a statue erected in its honor, nor heard a hymn dedicated to it. Pain is usually defined as "unpleasantness." Christians don't really know how to interpret pain. If you pinned them against the wall, or in the dark, secret moment, many Christians would probably concede that pain was God's mistake. God really should have worked harder and invented a better way of alerting us to the world's dangers. I am convinced that pain gets a lot of bad press. Perhaps we *should* see statues, hymns, and poems to pain. Up close, under a microscope, the pain network is seen in an entirely different dimension.

In our embarrassment over the problem of pain, we seem to have forgotten a central fact which was repeatedly brought to my attention by Dr. Paul Brand, a missionary surgeon who headed the rehabilitation branch of America's only leprosarium. "If I had one gift which I could give to people with leprosy, it would be the gift of pain," Dr. Brand said.

Pain itself, the hurt of pain, is a gift. After years of working with leprosy patients Dr. Brand learned to exult in the sensation of cutting a finger, turning an ankle, stepping into a too-hot bath. "Thank God for pain!" he says.

Doctors once believed the disease of leprosy caused the ulcers on hands and feet and face which eventually led to rotting flesh and the gradual loss of limbs. Mainly through Dr. Brand's research, it has been established that in ninety-nine percent of the cases, leprosy only *numbs* the extremities. The decay of flesh occurs solely because the warning system of pain is absent.

How does the decay happen? Visitors to rural villages in Africa and Asia have sometimes observed a horrible sight: a person with leprosy standing by the heavy iron cooking pot watching the potatoes. As they are done, without flinching he thrusts his arm deep into the scalding water and recovers the cooked potatoes. Dr. Brand found that abusive acts such as this were the chief cause of body deterioration. The potato-watching leprosy victim had felt no pain, but his skin blistered, his cells were destroyed and laid open to infection. Leprosy had not destroyed the tissue; it had merely removed the warning sensors that alerted him to danger.

On one occasion, as Dr. Brand was still formulating this radical theory, he tried to open the door of a little storeroom, but a rusty padlock would not yield to his pressure on the key. A leprosy patient, an undersized, malnourished ten-year-old, approached him, smiling.

"Let me try, sahib doctor," he offered and reached for the key. He closed his thumb and forefinger on the key and with a quick jerk of the hand turned it in the lock. Brand was dumbfounded. How could this weak youngster out-exert him? His eyes caught a tell-tale clue. Was that a drop of blood on the floor?

Upon examining the boy's fingers, Brand discovered the act of turning the key had slashed the finger open to the bone; skin and fat and joint were all exposed. Yet the boy was completely unaware of it! To him, the sensation of cutting a finger to the bone was no different than picking up a stone or turning a coin in his pocket.

The daily routines of life ground away at these patients' hands and feet, but without a warning system to alert them, they succumbed. If an ankle turned, tearing tendon and muscle, they would adjust and walk crookedly. If a rat chewed off a finger in the night, they would not discover it until the next morning. (In fact, Brand required his departing patients to take a cat home with them to prevent this common occurrence.)

His discovery revolutionized medicine's approach to leprosy. And it starkly illustrates why Paul Brand can say with utter sincerity, "Thank God for pain!" By definition, pain is unpleasant, so unpleasant as to *force* us to withdraw our finger from boiling water, lightning-fast. Yet it is that very quality which saves us from destruction. Unless the warning signal demands response, we might not heed it.

Just as physical pain is an early warning
system to the brain, it is a warning system
to the soul.

Brand's discovery in the physical realm closely parallels the moral argument for pain offered by C. S. Lewis in *The Problem of Pain.* Just as physical pain is an early warning system to the brain, it is a warning system to the soul. Pain is a megaphone of God which, sometimes murmuring, sometimes shouting, reminds us that something is wrong. It is a "rumor of transcendence" which convinces us the entire human condition is out of whack. We on earth are a rebel fortress, and every sting and every ache remind us.

We could (some people do) believe that the purpose of life here is to be comfortable. Enjoy yourself, build a nice home, engorge good food, have sex, live the good life. That's all there is. But the presence of suffering complicates that philosophy. It's much harder to believe that the world is here for my hedonistic fulfillment when a billion of its people go to bed starving each night. It's much harder to believe that the purpose of life is to feel good when I see people smashed on the freeway. If I try to escape the idea and merely enjoy life, suffering is there, haunting me, reminding me of how hollow life would be if this world were all I'd ever know.

Something is wrong with a life of wars and violence and insults. We need help. He who wants to be satisfied with this world, who wants to think the only reason for living is to enjoy a good life, must do so with cotton in his ears; the megaphone of pain is a loud one.

Pain, God's megaphone, can drive me away from faith. I can hate God for allowing such misery. Or, on the other hand, it can drive me to God. I can believe the promise that this world is not all there is, and take the chance that God is making a perfect place for those who follow him on pain-wracked earth.

There are two contributions to the problem of pain that hold true in any circumstance, whether healing or death ensues. The first is the simple fact of Jesus' coming. When God entered humanity, he saw and felt for himself what this world is like. Jesus took on the same kind of body you and I have. His nerve fibers were not bionic—they screamed with pain when they were misused. And above all, Jesus was surely misused. This fact of history can have a large effect on the fear and helpless despair of sufferers.

The scene of Christ's death, with the sharp spikes and the

wrenching thud as the cross was dropped in the ground, has been told so often that we, who shrink from a news story on the death of a race horse or of baby seals, do not flinch at its retelling. It was a bloody death, an execution quite unlike the quick, sterile ones we know today: gas chambers, electric chairs, hangings. This one stretched on for hours in front of a jeering crowd.

Jesus' death is the cornerstone of the Christian faith, the most important fact of his coming. You can't follow Jesus without confronting his death; the Gospels bulge with its details. He laid out a trail of hints and bold predictions about it throughout his ministry, predictions that were only understood after the thing had been done, when to the disciples the dream looked shattered. His life seemed prematurely wasted. His triumphant words from the night before surely must have cruelly haunted his followers as they watched him groan and twitch on the cross.

What possible contribution to the problem of pain could come from a religion based on an event like the crucifixion? Simply, we are not abandoned. Because Jesus came and took a place beside us, God fully understands. Dorothy Sayers says:

> For whatever reason God chose to make man as he is—limited and suffering and subject to sorrows and death—He had the honesty and courage to take His own medicine. Whatever game He is playing with His creation, He has kept His own rules and played fair. He can exact nothing from man that He has not exacted from Himself. He has Himself gone through the whole of human experience, from the trivial irritations of family life and the cramping restrictions of hard work and lack of money to the worst horrors of pain and humiliation, defeat, despair, and death. When He was a man, he played the man. He was born in poverty and died in disgrace and thought it well worthwhile.[1]

By taking it on himself, Jesus in a sense dignified pain. Of all the kinds of lives he could have lived, he chose a suffering one. Because of Jesus, I can never say about a person, "He must be suffering because of some sin he committed." Jesus, who did not sin, also felt pain. And I cannot say, "Suffering and death must mean God has forsaken us; he's left us alone to self-destruct." Because even though Jesus died, his death became the great victory of history, pulling man and God together. God made a supreme good out of that day. T. S. Eliot wrote in *Four Quartets:*

> The wounded surgeon plies the steel
> That questions the distempered part;
> Beneath the bleeding hands we feel
> The sharp compassion of the healer's art
> Resolving the enigma of the fever chart.

That uniquely Christian contribution is a memory. But there is another one—a hope. To the person with unrequited suffering, it is the most important contribution of all. Christ did not stay on the cross. After three days in a dark tomb, he was seen alive again. Alive! Could it be? His disciples couldn't believe it at first. But he came to them, letting them feel his new body. Christ brought us the possibility of an afterlife without pain and suffering. All our hurts are temporary.

By taking it on himself,
Jesus in a sense dignified pain.

In seventy years we can develop a host of ideas about how indifferent God appears to be about suffering. But is it reasonable to judge God and his plan for the universe by the swatch of time we spend on earth? Have we missed the perspective of the timelessness of the universe?

Who would complain if God allowed one hour of suffering in an entire lifetime of comfort? Yet we bitterly complain about a lifetime that includes suffering when that lifetime is a mere hour of eternity.

In the Christian scheme of things, this world and the time spent here are not all there is. Earth is a proving ground; a dot in eternity—but a very important dot, for Jesus said our destiny depends on our obedience here. Next time you want to cry out to God in anguished despair, blaming him for a miserable world, remember: less than one-millionth of the evidence has been presented, and that is being worked out under a rebel flag.

God is not deaf. God is as grieved by the world's trauma as you are. His only son died here. But God has promised to set things right.

Let history finish. Let the orchestra scratch out its last mournful warm-up note of discord before it bursts into the symphony. As Paul said, "In my opinion whatever we may have to go through now is less than nothing compared with the magnificent future God has planned for us. The whole creation is on tiptoe to see the wonderful sight of the sons of God coming into their own. . . .

"It is plain to anyone with eyes to see that at the present time all created life groans in a sort of universal travail. And it is plain, too, that we who have a foretaste of the Spirit are in a state of painful tension, while we wait for that redemption of our bodies which will mean that at last we have realized our full sonship in Him" (Rom. 8:18, 19, 22, 23, PHILLIPS).

As we look back on the speck of eternity that was the history of this planet, we will be impressed not by its importance, but by its smallness. From the viewpoint of the Andromeda Galaxy, the holo-caustic destruction of our entire solar system would be barely visible, a match flaring faintly in the distance, then imploding in permanent darkness. Yet for this burnt-out match, God sacrificed himself. Pain can be seen, as Berkouwer puts it, as the great "not yet" of eternity. It reminds us of where we are, and creates in us a thirst for where we will someday be.

Adapted from *Open Windows* © 1982 by Philip Yancey, published by Crossway Books. Used by permission of the author.

Philip Yancey is a prolific author and editor-at-large for *Christianity Today* magazine.

3

God's Plan A

JONI EARECKSON TADA

" . . . you meant evil against me, but God meant it
for good . . . " *Genesis 50:20*

There was a time when I was content to wade ankle-deep in the
things of God. But that was before I snapped my neck under the
weight of a dive into shallow water, and a severed spinal cord left my
body limp and useless. Permanent and total paralysis smashed me
up against the study of God. And in the wee, sleepless hours of my
early injury, I wrestled with questions about why and how this had
happened to me. This was no casual question-and-answer session
in a living room Bible study, nor was it a merely academic exercise.
I fought off claustrophobia with hard-hitting questions directed at
God: "Let me get this straight, God . . . when bad things happen,
who's behind them, you or the devil? Did you permit this or was this
your plan for me?"

It was in the hospital that I first read the book of Job, and
honestly I felt confused. The way I pictured God's role in my
accident was far different than what I read in Job's story. In Job
chapter 1, God makes it clear that he's in charge. Satan conspires to
use everything to cause Job misery so that he will turn his back on
God—from the Sabeans to the Chaldeans, from freak storms to fire

from the skies—but God is the one who ultimately grants the devil permission to make Job's life miserable.

I had reasoned that it was pure dumb luck that I happened to go to the beach that day. I thought it was the law of averages that the tide just happened to be low that day. I figured that if Satan and God were involved in my accident at all, then it must be that the devil had twisted God's arm for permission. I pictured God responding in a hesitant way, "Well, I guess it'll be okay for you to do such and such . . . but just this once, and please don't hurt her too much."

I reasoned that once God granted permission to Satan, he then nervously had to run behind him with a repair kit, patching up what Satan had ruined, mumbling to himself, "Oh great, now how am I going to work this for good?"

Worse yet, I thought that when I became disabled I had missed God's best for me, and that the Lord was then forced to go with some divine Plan B for my life.

I think this is the false picture many people have about the suffering in their lives. They assume that Satan's schemes throw a monkey wrench into God's plans, catching him off-guard, and presenting God with problems he wishes would have never happened.

But the truth is that God is infinitely more powerful than Satan. Satan is a created being, and a fallen one at that. And in the book of Job, God did not hesitantly and nervously grant permission to the devil to bring suffering into Job's life. Rather, God was the one who introduced the subject of Job to Satan. So who was ultimately in control? God was. And not only was God not frustrated or hindered by Satan's schemes, God actually intended to use the devil's deeds to serve his own ends and accomplish his own good purposes in Job's life.

Likewise, while the devil's motive in my disability was to shipwreck my faith by throwing a wheelchair in my way, I'm convinced that God's motive was to thwart the devil and use the wheelchair to change me and make me more like Christ through it all.

God is heaven-bent on inviting me to share in his joy, peace, and power. But there's a catch. God only shares his joy on his terms, and those terms call for us, in some measure, to suffer as his beloved Son did while on earth. "For to this you have been called, because Christ also suffered for you, leaving you an example, so that you might follow in his steps" (1 Pet. 2:21). Those steps lead us into the fellowship of Christ's sufferings where we become "like him in his death"; that is, we daily take up our cross and die *to* the sins he died *for* on his cross (Phil. 3:10; Luke 9:23).

God only shares his joy on his terms,
and those terms call for us to suffer as his
beloved Son did.

When suffering sandblasts us to the core, the true stuff of which we are made is revealed. Suffering lobs a hand-grenade into our self-centeredness, blasting our soul bare, so we can be better bonded to the Savior. Our afflictions help to make us holy. And we are never more like Christ, never more filled with his joy, peace, and power, than when sin is uprooted from our lives.

Does this mean God delights in my spinal cord injury? Was he rubbing his hands in glee when I took that dive off the raft into shallow water? Of course not. He may work "all things" together for my good, but that does not mean a spinal cord injury is, in itself, good (Rom. 8:28). God permits all sorts of things he doesn't approve of. In fact, in a world of evil and wickedness, he allows others to do what he would never do—he didn't steal Job's camels or entice the

Sabeans or Chaldeans to wreak havoc. Yet he was able to erect a "fence" around Satan's fury to bring ultimate good out of the devil's wickedness. As my friend and mentor, Steve Estes, once told me, "Satan may power the ship of evil, but God steers it to serve his own ends and purposes."

So I could ask, "Was my diving accident God's fault?" Although he is sovereign, no, it was not his fault. Or I could ask, "Was it an assault from the devil?" and say yes, it possibly was. Or I can press further, asking, "Was it part of living in a fallen, wicked world, and not the *direct* assault of either the devil or God?" This may be the most likely scenario, but whichever the schematic, I have the comfort and confidence that the entire matter was under God's overarching decrees, and that nothing happens in my life outside his loving plans for me.

Besides, how God allowed for my accident to happen is not the point. The point is, my suffering has taught me to "be done with sin," putting behind me the peevish, small-minded, self-focused "Joni" to mature into the "Joni" he has destined me to be, honed and polished by years of quadriplegia (1 Pet. 4:1).

I'm not saying it's easy. Actually, it's getting harder. These thin, tired bones are beginning to bend under the weight of decades of paralysis. But I have to remember that the core of God's plan is to rescue me from sin, even up to my dying breath. My pain and discomfort are not his ultimate focus. He cares about these things, but they are merely symptoms of the real problem. God cares most, not about making my life happy, healthy, and free of trouble, but about teaching me to hate my transgressions and to keep growing in the grace and knowledge of Jesus. God lets me continue to feel sin's sting through suffering while I'm heading for heaven, constantly reminding me of what I am being delivered from, exposing sin for the poison it is.

In short, one form of evil—suffering—is turned on its head to defeat another form of evil—my sin—all to the praise of God's wisdom and glory! Is the cost too great? Is the price of pain too high? Not when you consider that "this light momentary affliction is preparing for us an eternal weight of glory beyond all comparison" (2 Cor. 4:17).

One day God will close the curtain on evil and, with it, all suffering and sorrow. Until then, I'll keep remembering something else Steve Estes once told me as he rested his hand on my wheelchair: "God permits what he hates to accomplish what he loves." I can smile knowing God is accomplishing what he loves in my life—Christ in me, the hope of glory. And this is no Plan B for my life, but his good and loving Plan A.

Scripture quotations are from the ESV® Bible (*The Holy Bible, English Standard Version®*).

4

When We Don't Know Why, We Trust God Who Knows Why

OS GUINNESS

And about the ninth hour Jesus cried out with a loud voice, saying, "Eli, Eli, lema sabachthani?" that is, "My God, my God, why have you forsaken me?" *Matthew 27:46*

Suffering is the most acute trial that faith can face, and the questions it raises are the sharpest, the most insistent, and the most damaging that faith will meet. Can faith bear the pain and still trust God, suspending judgment and resting in the knowledge that God is there, God is good, and God knows best? Or will the pain be so great that only meaning will make it endurable so that reason must be pressed further and further and judgments must be made?

To suffer is one thing, to suffer without meaning is another, but to suffer and choose not to press for any meaning is worst of all. Yet that is the suicidal submission that faith's suspension of judgment seems to involve.

There are times when we see glimpses of God's ways but not enough to allow us to make true conclusions about what he is doing and why. Yet we cannot resist jumping to conclusions anyway. Then, being insistent as well as inquisitive, we refuse to suspend judgment, and our wrong conclusions so misrepresent God that we end by doubting him. But if the Christian's faith is to be itself and let God be God at such times, it must suspend judgment and say, "Father, I do not understand you, but I trust you."

The Christian's faith must suspend judgment and say, "Father, I do not understand you, but I trust you."

Notice what this means. Christians do not say, "I do not understand you at all, but I trust you anyway." Rather we say, "I do not understand you *in this situation,* but I *understand why I trust you anyway.* Therefore I can trust that you understand even though I don't."

If we do not know why we trust God in the beginning, then we will always need to know exactly what God is doing in order to trust him. Failing to grasp that, we may not be able to continue trusting him, for anything we do not understand may count decisively against what we are able to trust.

If, on the other hand, we do know why we trust God, we will be able to trust him in situations where we do not understand what he is doing. It may be mystery to us, but mystery is only inscrutable; what would be insufferable is absurdity. Faith does not know why in terms of the immediate, but it knows why it trusts God who knows why in terms of the ultimate.

If all religious issues were boiled down to their essence, there would be two inescapable questions: Is God there? And, is God good? Our view of the existence of God and the character of God are the truths that determine all our other answers.

For Christians, the answer to both questions "How may I be

sure that God is there and that God is good?" is answered satisfactorily only in Jesus Christ. Any "proof" of God's existence or argument in favor of his goodness that ends elsewhere is bound to be inconclusive or wrong. However cogent and compelling they may seem as arguments, in the long run they will prove both intellectually weak and emotionally unsatisfying, and there is nothing like suffering to show up this flaw.

The test of suffering reveals whether our "knowing why" is an irreducible bedrock conviction grounded in the revelation of God in Jesus Christ, or whether our faith is resting to any degree on what is not bedrock but sand.

We suffer, we look up, we cry out, we pray, we tear our hearts out, but there is no answer. The heavens are brass, the gates are locked, the phone is busy, and in the ringing nothingness of silence we wonder if God was ever there. "Be not deaf to my cry," says the psalmist, "lest, if thou answer me with silence, I become like those who go down to the abyss."

What is difficult enough for believers who know why they trust God is unbearable for believers who are uncertain or for nominal believers. No generation bears more eloquent testimony to this than our own. In his play *The Devil and the Good Lord,* Jean-Paul Sartre portrays Goetz, a butchering soldier-turned-saint who grows disillusioned by his spiritual ineffectiveness and God's silence. Eventually he wonders if his creed is true or whether it is only his own voice shouting out loud to cover God's silence. Finally he bursts out,

> I prayed, I demanded a sign. I sent messages to Heaven, no reply. Heaven ignored my very name. Each minute I wonder what I could BE in the eyes of God. Now I know the answer: nothing. God does not see me, God does not hear me, God does not know me. You see this emptiness over our heads? That is God. You see this gap in the

door? It is God. You see that hole in the ground? That is God again. Silence is God. Absence is God. God is the loneliness of man.[1]

This terrible cry of uncertainty that trails off into unbelief is echoed many times in modern drama and literature. Increasingly, especially after Auschwitz, the problem of justice in an evil world is approached from the moral position that declares the bystander to be guilty—and therefore indicts God as the eternal bystander.

But literary examples fade in comparison with the eyewitness descriptions of those who have faced the silence of God in real experience. One example is Nobel Laureate Elie Wiesel's account of Auschwitz in *Night*. A Hungarian-born Jew, Elie Wiesel was a survivor of both Auschwitz and Buchenwald, and his book is a searing account of a small boy encountering unmasked evil.

> Never shall I forget that night, the first night in camp, which has turned my life into one long night, seven times cursed and seven times sealed. . . . Never shall I forget those flames which consumed my faith forever. Never shall I forget that nocturnal silence which deprived me, for all eternity, of the desire to live. Never shall I forget those moments which murdered my God and my soul and turned my dream to dust. Never shall I forget these things, even if I am condemned to live as long as God Himself. Never.[2]

And what of the Christian? Are we different because our courage is greater or our theological explanations more nimble? Far from it. We too recoil from such a snake pit of evil. We feel the same pain, the same agony, the same questions, the same silence. We do not know why either, but (and here alone is the difference) we know why we trust God who knows why.

And how is this? Because of another Jew, a Jew not in his youth, but in his prime, not under compulsion but freely, who took on himself the full desolation of God's silence so that after suffering in

our place he might restore us to his Father, that then v
sure that God is there and God is good.

For the Christian, the cry of Jesus, "My God, my
hast thou forsaken me?" will always have depths of meaning that
the human mind can never fathom. But one thing at least it means.
None of us can sink so low that God has not gone lower still. As
C. S. Lewis puts it, "Sometimes it is hard not to say 'God forgive
God.' Sometimes it is hard to say so much. But if our faith is true,
He didn't. He crucified him."[3]

Martin Luther once read the story of Abraham's sacrifice of Isaac
in his family devotions. When he had finished, his wife Katie said
simply, "I do not believe it. God would not have treated his son like
that."

"But, Katie," Luther answered, "he did."[4]

 Doubts about the Father are silenced
in the Son.

This is how doubts about the Father are silenced in the Son.
God may become remote to us in times of suffering—unless he is
"the God and Father of our Lord Jesus Christ." Do you catch the
intimacy in that little giveaway description of God? Jesus was known
and loved by the disciples. To them he was *our* Lord Jesus Christ.
They had followed him, lived with him, learned from him. They
loved him, and they would lay down their lives for him. But who was
God whom they had never seen? Quite simply he was "Jesus Christ's
Father," and so they called him "the God, and Father of our Lord
Jesus Christ." Didn't Jesus himself say, "Go to my brothers, and tell
them that I am now ascending to my Father and your Father, my

God and your God"? Hadn't he taught them to pray "Our Father in heaven"?

So the truth of the Incarnation is not just good theology; it is practical comfort and assurance. Jesus identifies with us in our humanity, and now we know that God is for us in Christ. He can be trusted. He went through torture too. When we see Jesus on the cross we can come to trust God with an unutterable trust that never for a moment considers he will not stand by us in our sufferings.

Adapted from *God in the Dark* by Os Guinness ©1996 by Os Guinness, published by Crossway Books.

Os Guinness is a scholar and lecturer and cofounder of the Trinity Forum.

5

Is There Such a Thing as Senseless Tragedy?

R. C. SPROUL

And we know that for those who love God all things
work together for good, for those who are called
according to his purpose. *Romans 8:28*

I am especially concerned when events are described as a "senseless tragedy." If we look closely at the phrase, it becomes obvious that "senseless tragedy" is an oxymoron. It is a self-contradictory statement, a phrase that makes no sense. For something to be defined as "tragic" there first must be some standard of good for it to be deemed tragic over against. But if things happen in a way that is "senseless," there cannot be anything that is either a tragedy or a blessing. Each event would simply be meaningless.

The word "tragedy" presupposes some kind of order or purpose in the world. If the world has purpose and order, then all that occurs in it is meaningful in some respect. The idea of a "senseless tragedy" represents a worldview that is completely incompatible with Christian thought. It assumes that something happens without purpose or without meaning. If God is God and if he is a God of providence, if he is truly sovereign, then nothing ever happens that is ultimately senseless. Things may appear to be without purpose or meaning. Their ultimate purpose might elude us for the present. Yet if we fail to see purpose in what happens, we must remember that our view of things is limited by our earthly perspective.

An important slogan in theology is *finitum non capax infiniti*. This means, "the finite cannot grasp the infinite." The limit of our comprehension is the earthly perspective. We do not have the ability to see things *sub specie aeternitatis*—"from the eternal perspective."

The eternal perspective belongs to God. He is the infinite One, whose understanding is likewise infinite. If God is truly sovereign—if he rules over all things—then nothing that ever happens is senseless. Events can be senseless only if: (1) God is not sovereign over them; or (2) he himself is senseless. What would be *truly* senseless is a view of God that regards him either as not sovereign or as senseless.

If God is truly sovereign—if he rules over all things—then nothing that ever happens is senseless.

But what about the reality of tragedy? Even in tragedies that are not senseless, are they not still tragic? First we must define the term "tragedy." Apart from its reference to a particular form of drama, the term, according to the dictionary, refers to that which may be called "a disastrous event," a "calamity," or a "severe misfortune."

If we look at the disasters that befell Joseph in the Old Testament, we see that what seemed tragic in the short term was actually a blessing in the long term. We remember Joseph's words to his brothers:

"Do not be afraid, for am I in the place of God? But as for you, you meant evil against me; but God meant it for good, in order to bring it about as it is this day, to save many people alive." (Gen. 50:19–20)

Joseph's "tragedy" was ordained of God for a redemptive purpose. It appeared as a senseless tragedy while in actuality it was a divinely appointed event with a redemptive purpose.

That is seen nowhere more clearly than in the cross. Luke records an event that took place after Jesus' crucifixion:

Now behold, two of them were traveling that same day to a village called Emmaus, which was seven miles from Jerusalem. And they talked together of all these things which had happened. So it was, while they conversed and reasoned, that Jesus Himself drew near and went with them. But their eyes were restrained, so that they did not know Him.

And He said to them, "What kind of conversation is this that you have with one another as you walk and are sad?"

Then the one whose name was Cleopas answered and said to Him, "Are You the only stranger in Jerusalem, and have You not known the things which happened there in these days?"

And He said to them, "What things?"

So they said to Him, "The things concerning Jesus of Nazareth, who was a Prophet mighty in deed and word before God and all the people, and how the chief priests and our rulers delivered Him to be condemned to death, and crucified Him. But we were hoping that it was He who was going to redeem Israel. Indeed, besides all this, today is the third day since these things happened. Yes, and certain women of our company, who arrived at the tomb early, astonished us. When they did not find His body, they came saying that they had also seen a vision of angels who said He was alive. And certain of those who were with us went to the tomb and found it just as the women had said; but Him they did not see."

Then He said to them, "O foolish ones, and slow of heart to believe in all that the prophets have spoken! Ought not the Christ to have suffered these things and to enter into His glory?" And beginning at Moses and all the Prophets, He expounded to them in all the Scriptures the things concerning Himself. (Luke 24:13–27)

We notice in this conversation that the two men walking with Jesus were described as being sad. When Jesus asked them why they were sad, they recounted to him the events of the crucifixion. They expressed the poignant feeling, "But we were hoping that it was He who was going to redeem Israel" (Luke 24:21). At the death of Jesus, these men had experienced the utter destruction of their hope. The hope they had placed in Jesus was crushed. The cross had shattered it. To them, at this time, the cross represented the supreme tragedy. It made their previous devotion to Jesus appear to be "senseless."

The hope they expressed was for redemption. They trusted that Jesus was the One who was going to redeem Israel. At first glance, nothing seemed to be further from a redemptive act than Jesus' death on the cross. Pilate certainly did not intend the cross as an act of redemption. The crowds who clamored for Christ's blood did not view the cross as redemptive. And it is obvious that these disciples, looking back on that terrible event, didn't view it that way either.

The cross was not a senseless tragedy,
but the most important redemptive act in
human history.

Jesus went to the Scripture to show these men, whom he described as "foolish" and "slow of heart to believe," that the Bible made it clear that the cross was not a senseless tragedy, but the most important redemptive act in human history. For all who down through the ages have put their trust in Jesus, the cross is their highest blessing as it turns Black Friday into Good Friday.

Romans 8:28 summarizes it beautifully: "And we know th things work together for good to those who love God, to those who are the called according to His purpose."

This verse is not merely a biblical expression of comfort for those who suffer affliction. It is far more than that. It is a radical *credo* for the Christian worldview. It represents the absolute triumph of divine purpose over all alleged acts of chaos. It erases "misfortune" from the vocabulary of the Christian.

God, in his providence, has the power and the will to work *all things* together for good for his people. This does not mean that everything that happens to us is, in itself, good. Really bad things do happen to us. But they are only proximately bad; they are never ultimately bad. That is, they are bad only in the short (proximate) term, never in the long term. Because of the triumph of God's goodness in all things, he is able to bring good for us out of the bad. He turns our tragedies into supreme blessings.

Adapted from *When Worlds Collide: Where Is God?* ©2002 by R. C. Sproul, published by Crossway Books.

R. C. Sproul is a theologian and pastor, and is chairman of Ligonier Ministries.

Scripture quotations are from the *New King James Version* of the Bible.

6

Illumined by the Light of Divine Providence

JOHN CALVIN

In him we have obtained an inheritance, having been predestined according to the purpose of him who works all things according to the counsel of his will, so that we who were the first to hope in Christ might be to the praise of his glory. *Ephesians 1:11–12*

The Christian, being most fully persuaded, that all things come to pass by the dispensation of God, and that nothing happens fortuitously, will always direct his eye to him as the principal cause of events, at the same time paying due regard to inferior causes in their own place. Next, he will have no doubt that a special providence is awake for his preservation, and will not suffer anything to happen that will not turn to his good and safety. But as its business is first with men and then with the other creatures, he will feel assured that the providence of God reigns over both. In regard to men, good as well as bad, he will acknowledge that their counsels, wishes, aims and faculties are so under his hand, that he has full power to turn them in whatever direction, and constrain them as often as he pleases.

49

This knowledge is necessarily followed by gratitude in prosperity, patience in adversity, and incredible security for the time to come. Every thing, therefore, which turns out prosperous and according to his wish, the Christian will ascribe entirely to God, whether he has experienced his beneficence through the instrumentality of men, or been aided by inanimate creatures. For he will thus consider with himself: Certainly it was the Lord that disposed the minds of these people in my favor, attaching them to me so as to make them the instruments of his kindness. In an abundant harvest he will think that it is the Lord who listens to the heaven, that the heaven may listen to the earth, and the earth herself to her own offspring; in other cases, he will have no doubt that he owes all his prosperity to the divine blessing, and, admonished by so many circumstances, will feel it impossible to be ungrateful.

If any thing adverse befalls him, he will forthwith raise his mind to God, whose hand is most effectual in impressing us with patience and placid moderation of mind. Had Joseph kept his thoughts fixed on the treachery of his brethren, he never could have resumed fraternal affection for them. But turning toward the Lord, he forgot the injury, and was so inclined to mildness and mercy, that he even voluntarily comforts his brethren, telling them, "Be not grieved nor angry with yourselves that ye sold me hither; for God did send me before you to preserve life." "As for you, ye thought evil against me; but God meant it unto good" (Gen. 45:5; 50:20). Had Job turned to the Chaldees, by whom he was plundered, he should instantly have been fired with revenge, but recognizing the work of the Lord, he solaces himself with this most beautiful sentiment: "The Lord gave, and the Lord has taken away; blessed be the name of the Lord" (Job 1:21). So when David was assailed by Shimei with stones and curses, had he immediately fixed his eyes on the man, he would have urged his people to retaliate the injury; but perceiving that he acts not without an impulse from the Lord, he rather calms them. "So let him curse," says he, "because the Lord has said unto him, Curse David." With the same bridle he elsewhere curbs the excess of his grief, "I was dumb, I opened not my mouth, because thou didst it" (Ps. 39:9).

If there is no more effectual remedy for anger and impatience, he assuredly has not made little progress who has learned so to meditate on Divine Providence, as to be able always to bring his mind to this, The Lord willed it, it must therefore be borne; not only because it is unlawful to strive with him, but because he wills nothing that is not just and befitting. The whole comes to this. When unjustly assailed by men, overlooking their malice (which could only aggravate our grief, and whet our minds for vengeance), let us remember to ascend to God, and learn to hold it for certain, that whatever an enemy wickedly committed against us was permitted, and sent by his righteous dispensation. Paul, in order to suppress our desire to retaliate injuries, wisely reminds us that we wrestle not with flesh and blood, but with our spiritual enemy the devil, that we may prepare for the contest (Eph. 6:12).

The Lord willed it, it must therefore be borne;
not only because it is unlawful to strive
with him, but because he wills nothing that
is not just and befitting.

But to calm all the impulses of passion, the most useful consideration is, that God arms the devil, as well as all the wicked, for conflict, and sits as umpire, that he may exercise our patience. But if the disasters and miseries which press us happen without the agency of men, let us call to mind the doctrine of the Law (Deut. 28:1), that all prosperity has its source in the blessing of God, that all adversity is his curse. And let us tremble at the dreadful denunciation, "And if ye will not be reformed by these things, but will walk contrary unto me; then will I also walk contrary unto you" (Lev. 26:23–24). These words condemn our torpor, when, according to our carnal sense, deeming that whatever happens in any way is fortuitous, we are neither animated by the kindness of God to worship him, nor by his scourge stimulated to repentance. And it is for this reason that Jeremiah (Lam. 3:38), and Amos (Amos 3:6), expostulated bitterly with the Jews, for not believing that good as well as evil was produced by the command of God. To the same effect are the words in Isaiah, "I form the light and create darkness: I make peace and create evil. I the Lord do all these things" (Isa. 45:7).

The Christian's mind will always be fixed on the Providence of God alone, and no consideration of present circumstances will be allowed to withdraw him from the steady contemplation of it. Thus Joab, while he acknowledges that the issue of the battle is entirely in the hand of God, does not therefore become inactive, but strenuously proceeds with what belongs to his proper calling, "Be of good courage," says he, "and let us play the men for our people, and for the cities of our God; and the Lord do that which seemeth him good," (2 Sam. 10:12). The same conviction keeping us free from rashness and false confidence, will stimulate us to constant prayer, while at the same time filling our minds with good hope, it will enable us to feel secure, and bid defiance to all the dangers by which we are surrounded.

When once the light of Divine Providence has illumined the believer's soul, he is relieved and set free, not only from the extreme fear and anxiety which formerly oppressed him, but from all care. For as he justly shudders at the idea of chance, so he can confidently commit himself to God. This, I say, is his comfort, that his heavenly Father so embraces all things under his power—so governs them at will by his nod—so regulates them by his wisdom, that nothing takes place save according to his appointment; that received into his favour, and entrusted to the care of his angels neither fire, nor water, nor sword, can do him harm, except in so far as God their master is pleased to permit.

> Ignorance of Providence is the greatest
> of all miseries, and the knowledge of it
> the highest happiness.

How comes it, I ask, that their confidence never fails, but just that while the world apparently revolves at random, they know that God is every where at work, and feel assured that his work will be their safety? When assailed by the devil and wicked men, were they not confirmed by remembering and meditating on Providence, they should, of necessity, forthwith despond. But when they call to mind that the devil, and the whole train of the ungodly, are, in all directions, held in by the hand of God as with a bridle, so that they can neither conceive any mischief, nor plan what they have conceived, nor how much soever they may have planned, move a single finger to perpetrate, unless in so far as he permits, nay, unless in so far as he commands; that they are not only bound by his fetters, but are even forced to do him service—when the godly think of all these things they have ample sources of consolation. For, as it belongs to the Lord to arm the fury of such foes and turn and destine it at pleasure, so it is his also to determine the measure and the end, so as to prevent them from breaking loose and wantoning as they list.

Give heed, and you will at once perceive that ignorance of Providence is the greatest of all miseries, and the knowledge of it the highest happiness.

Adapted from *Institutes of the Christian Religion* by John Calvin, translated by Henry Beveridge in 1845 for the Calvin Translation Society.

John Calvin (1509–1564) was an influential French theologian and pastor during the Protestant Reformation.

7

A Profound Answer to the Pressing Question, "Why?"

WILSON BENTON JR.

O LORD, how long shall I cry for help,
and you will not hear?
Or cry to you "Violence!" and you will not save?
Why do you make me see iniquity, and why do you
idly look at wrong?

Habakkuk 1:2–3

It does seem that man is born to question, because he begins that exercise so early in his earthly pilgrimage. There is the innocent, incessant, inquisitive, *why? why? why?* of a three-year old. There is the nagging, whining, complaining, *why? why? why?* of a nine-year-old. Then there's the haughty, challenging, rebellious, *why? why? why?* of a fifteen-year-old.

Because God is our Father and we are his children, we find ourselves asking him those same kinds of questions. Sometimes there is on our part an innocent and inquisitive why. We wonder why God did things the way he did them, or why he does them the way he does them now.

If we are honest with ourselves we will admit that sometimes there is in our heart, if not on our lips, that bitter "why?" That nagging, complaining, whining "why?" *Why, God? Why does my little house of cards always collapse? Why is it that my plans are always frustrated? Why is it that I am the one that always seems to be disappointed in life?*

And if we are really honest, we will admit that sometimes there is formulated in our consciousness, if it's never expressed in conversation, that arrogant "why?", that haughty, challenging, rebellious "why?" *Why, God? What right have you to treat me like this?*

It's at this point that we feel a kinship with the Old Testament prophet Habakkuk. We feel that he knows us and we know him because he dares to ask God the very same questions that we want to ask God. And amazingly, God answers him. And in answering Habakkuk, God answers us.

The conversation begins with a question from Habakkuk: "How long, O Lord, am I going to cry to you for help before you answer me? Lord, how long before you're going to thunder from heaven with a voice of judgment against the sin of this land?" Habakkuk is frustrated over the apparent superiority of evil. It seems that everywhere he looks, the sinfulness of sin is stronger than the goodness of good. Everywhere he looks the forces that work for order are at the mercy of the forces that work for disorder. He wants to know why the wicked prosper and the righteous suffer.

And God comes to answer Habakkuk's question. He says, "Habakkuk, you're concerned because you think the wicked in your land will go unpunished. Let me assure you that is not the case. I'm going to punish the wicked in your land. I'm going to raise up Nebuchadnezzar, that great warlord of the Babylonians, and he is going to bring that terrible, horrible, cruel host of his against your nation to conquer them." Then God paints an awful scene of violence, saying that the Chaldean's horses are swifter than leopards, their men are more cruel than a pack of evening wolves. No fortified city can stand in their way; they are going to dwell in places and houses that are not their own. They're coming to crush the evil all around Habakkuk.

I suppose there is some small word of comfort in there, but there was no word of comfort for Habakkuk. In fact, God's answer to his first question raised an even greater question in his mind. And he cried, "Wait, Lord, you can't do that! You can't send the Babylonians here to punish your own people! Lord, I know we are sinful, I just confessed the sin of my land. But Lord, as sinful as we are, we are not as sinful as the Babylonians. As much as we may have turned from your law, we are not as pagan as Nebuchadnezzar and his host of soldiers. Lord, you can't use them to punish us. How can you allow the more wicked to punish the less wicked?"

The bottom line of Habakkuk's question is really this: *How can you, a holy God, use evil to accomplish good?* That's the question we have too. How can a loving, holy, righteous, gracious, merciful God ever use anything evil, sinful, wicked, or tragic to accomplish good in the lives of his people?

But we've not really felt the force of that question until we bring it home like Habakkuk must have. "Lord, you're saying *my* wife may be killed, *my* children may be marched into captivity? Lord, you're saying *I* may be killed? *I* may be marched into captivity? Lord, I'm your prophet. I'm your servant. I'm the one who's been concerned about the iniquity in our land, and now you're telling me that when punishment comes it may be indiscriminate? I myself may be the victim of that punishment when you know, Lord, I love you and I want your name honored? O God, why me?"

Are you honest enough to admit that you've asked that question too? *God, why has this come my way?* That's the force of Habakkuk's question.

God is not offended by our honest, legitimate questions about the way he does things. He's not in any way put off by our inquiries concerning his plan and purpose for our lives personally. And so he comes to deal with Habakkuk graciously and answer Habakkuk's question. In fact he gives him two answers. He gives him a partial answer and then he gives him a profound answer. He says, "Habakkuk, don't think my using Nebuchadnezzar excuses him from his own judgment to come. When I have used the Chaldeans to scourge my people, I will take that rod and break it into a thousand pieces and the judgment I dispense upon Nebuchadnezzar will be far greater than any judgment I use him to dispense on my own people."

But that was just a partial answer to Habakkuk's question. Habakkuk's deeper question, and our deeper question, concerns not the circumstances in which we find ourselves, but the character of God in those circumstances. You see our basic question has to do with the person of God and the plan of God for our lives and the power of God to work in our world.

It's the most profound answer God could
have given Habakkuk and it's just this:
"The just shall live by faith."

The question still stands: Lord, how can you use anything evil to accomplish good in the lives of your people? And God answers that question not with a partial answer, but with a profound answer. It's the most profound answer God could have given Habakkuk and it's just this: "The just shall live by faith" (Hab. 2:4).

And you say, *what? What's that got to do with it? I can identify* with Habakkuk as he flings his complaints into the face of God, but what in the world does the just living by faith have to do with these questions?

Everything. It's the most profound answer that God could have given.

God says, "Habakkuk, you want to know how I, as a holy God, can use evil to accomplish good. Even if I chose to explain to you how I do that, you could not comprehend it. Habakkuk, you must realize that you are one person living in one place at one point in time, and even if I chose to reveal to you my all-inclusive, overarching plan for the entire universe, you could not understand it. You are finite. But Habakkuk, you can believe that I understand how it all fits together. Habakkuk, you don't know what I'm doing, but Habakkuk, you can believe that *I know* what I'm doing. Even though you don't understand how good can come of this, you can believe that I understand how I am using all of this for your good. *The just shall live by faith.*"

You are one person living at one place, at one point in time and even if God chose to explain to you how all of the pieces of his giant puzzle are fitting together in a manner consistent with his own righteous and holy and gracious nature, so that he may faithfully fulfill his promise in your life and work everything that happens to you for your good, you couldn't understand it. But you can believe that God understands it. And you can believe that God is loving enough, and powerful enough, and wise enough, and gracious enough, and faithful enough to you to do what he says when he promises to work everything for your good.

We have something that Habakkuk did not have, a perspective that is ours that he did not possess, because we live on this side of the cross. What is the greatest tragedy this world has ever seen? What is the worst crime that has ever been committed? What is the most horrible thing that has ever happened in the history of mankind? Was it not the crucifixion of the only good, righteous, perfect man that ever lived? Of course. Did God bring anything good out of that evil event? What a foolish question for me to ask. Out of the worst thing that ever happened in the world, God brought the greatest triumph ever known in this world—your salvation and my salvation, the deliverance of all of his people. Our holy, righteous God used that awful, evil, horrible, terrible thing, the crucifixion of his own Son, to bring forth the greatest good this world has ever known.

> We have something that Habakkuk did
> not have, a perspective that is ours that he
> did not possess, because we live on
> this side of the cross.

Habakkuk responds to God's profound answer to his question by saying, "Yes, I want to live by faith," and so he expresses his faith in God's *sovereign power*. Habakkuk says, "The LORD is in his holy temple: let all the earth keep silence before him." What's he saying? Simply this: *No more questions, God. No more questions. God, I know you are on the throne. Wickedness doesn't reign supreme. The illegal and the immoral in this land are not in charge, you are still in charge. I'm glad you are in charge, and Lord, I acknowledge the fact that you are in control of my own personal circumstances. I'll be silent. No more questions, the Lord is in his holy temple and he is watching over me. He is the sovereign Lord of history and he is the sovereign Lord of my history.*

And in addition to expressing his faith in God's sovereign

power, Habakkuk expressed his faith in God's *sustaining power*. Habakkuk lived in an agricultural economy and God had said, "Your economy is going to be destroyed. Life as you know it, Habakkuk, is going down the tube. You are not going to have the necessities of life anymore. Listen, Habakkuk, it's going to be worse than you imagine."

What's Habakkuk's response to God's revelation? "Although the fig tree does not blossom, there are no grapes on the vine, no olive crop, the fields produce no food, there are no sheep in the pen, no cattle in the stalls, yet will I rejoice in the Lord, I will find joy in the God of my salvation."

Habakkuk is saying, "God, I really can walk by faith and not by sight. I don't know what you are doing but I trust your sustaining power."

Perhaps the greatest element of Habakkuk's testimony is that he expresses his faith in God's *saving power*. He says, "Lord, even if I lose my life in this holocaust, not just my goods, not just my home, not my job, not my family, Lord, if I am destroyed I still put my faith in you, the God of my salvation. If everything as I know it here, including life itself, is snuffed out, Lord, you've promised to make my feet like the deer's feet and take me to the high place of heaven itself."

What more could we ask for? What more could we want? What more could God promise in the face of all of our questions? We put our faith in the sovereign power of God, and in the sustaining power of God. We trust that God will provide, and if he doesn't, we put our faith in the saving power of God, knowing that he will take us unto himself. By God's grace we can say, "The answer to all of my questions is just this: The just shall live by faith."

Adapted from the sermon, "O God, Why Me?" by Dr. Wilson Benton. Used by permission.

Dr. Wilson Benton is a pastor in the Presbyterian Church of America where over the course of his career he has served not only as senior pastor but also as moderator of the PCA 20th General Assembly, chairman of the Committee for Mission to North America, and chairman of the Committee for Reformed University Ministries.

Scripture quotations are from the *King James Version* of the Bible.

8

Bearing Suffering

DIETRICH BONHOEFFER

Calling the crowd to him with his disciples, he said
to them, "If anyone would come after me, let him deny
himself and take up his cross and follow me." *Mark 8:34*

In denying Christ Peter said, "I do not know the man" (Matt.
26:74). Those who follow Christ must say that to themselves. Self-
denial means knowing only Christ, no longer knowing oneself. It
means no longer seeing oneself, only him who is going ahead, no
longer seeing the way which is too difficult for us. Self-denial says
only: he is going ahead; hold fast to him.

The grace of Jesus is evident in his preparing his disciples for
taking up their cross by speaking first of self-denial. Only when we
have really forgotten ourselves completely, when we really no longer
know ourselves, only then are we ready to take up the cross for his
sake. When we know only him, then we also no longer know the
pain of our own cross. Then we see only him. If Jesus had not been
so gracious in preparing us for this word, then we could not bear it.
But this way he has made us capable of hearing this hard word as
grace. It meets us in the joy of discipleship, and confirms us in it.

The cross is neither misfortune nor harsh fate. Instead, it is that
suffering which comes from our allegiance to Jesus Christ alone. The

cross is not random suffering, but necessary suffering. The cross is not suffering that stems from natural existence; it is suffering that comes from being Christian. The essence of the cross is not suffering alone; it is suffering and being rejected. Strictly speaking, it is being rejected for the sake of Jesus Christ, not for the sake of any other attitude or confession.

The cross is not random suffering, but necessary suffering.

From the beginning, it lies there ready. They need only take it up. But so that no one presumes to seek out some cross or arbitrarily search for some suffering, Jesus says, they each have *their* own cross ready, assigned by God and measured to fit.[1] They must all bear the suffering and rejection measured out to each of them. Everyone gets a different amount. God honors some with great suffering and grants them the grace of martyrdom, while others are not tempted beyond their strength. But in every case, it is the one cross. It is laid on every Christian.

Discipleship is being bound to the suffering Christ. That is why Christian suffering is not disconcerting. Instead, it is nothing but grace and joy. The acts of the church's first martyrs give witness that Christ transfigures the moment of greatest suffering for his followers through the indescribable certainty of his nearness and communion. In the middle of the most terrible torment that the disciples bore for their Lord's sake, they experienced the greatest joy and blessedness of his community. Bearing the cross proved to be for them the only way to overcome suffering. But this is true for all who follow Christ, because it was true for Christ himself.

"And going a little farther, [Jesus] threw himself on the ground and prayed, 'My Father, if it is possible, let this cup pass from me; yet not what I want but what you want.' . . . Again he went away for the second time and prayed, 'My Father, if this cannot pass unless I drink it, your will be done'" (Matt. 26:39, 42).

Jesus prays to the Father that the cup pass from him, and the Father hears the Son's prayer. The cup of suffering will pass from Jesus, but only by his drinking it. When Jesus kneels in Gethsemane the second time, he knows that the cup will pass by his accepting the suffering. Only by bearing the suffering will he overcome and conquer it. His cross is the triumph over suffering.

Suffering is distance from God. That is why someone who is in communion with God cannot suffer. Jesus affirmed this Old Testament testimony.[2] That is why he takes the suffering of the whole world onto himself and overcomes it. He bears the whole distance from God. Drinking the cup is what makes it pass from him. In order to overcome the suffering of the world Jesus must drink it to the dregs. Indeed suffering remains distance from God, but in community with the suffering of Jesus Christ, suffering is overcome by suffering. Communion with God is granted precisely in suffering.

Suffering must be borne in order for it to pass. Either the world must bear it and be crushed by it, or it falls on Christ and is overcome in him. That is how Christ suffers as vicarious representative for the world. Only his suffering brings salvation. But the church-community itself knows now that the world's suffering seeks a bearer. So in following Christ, the suffering falls upon it, and it bears the suffering while being borne by Christ. The community of Jesus Christ vicariously represents the world before God by following Christ under the cross.

God is a God who bears. The Son of God bore our flesh. He therefore bore the cross. He bore all our sins and attained reconciliation by his bearing. That is why disciples are called to bear what is put on them.

Suffering must be borne in order for it to pass. Either the world must bear it and be crushed by it, or it falls on Christ and is overcome in him.

Bearing constitutes being a Christian. Just as Christ maintains his communion with the Father by bearing according to the Father's will, so the disciples' bearing constitutes their community with Christ. People can shake off the burdens laid on them. But doing so does not free them at all from their burdens. Instead, it loads them with a heavier, more unbearable burden. They bear the self-chosen yoke of their own selves. Jesus called all who are laden with various sufferings and burdens to throw off their yokes and to take his yoke upon themselves. His yoke is easy, and his burden is light (Matt. 11:30). His yoke and his burden is the cross. Bearing the cross does not bring misery and despair. Rather, it provides refreshment and peace for our souls; it is our greatest joy. Here we are no longer laden with self-made laws and burdens, but with the yoke of him who knows us and who himself goes with us under the same yoke. Under his yoke we are assured of his nearness and communion. It is he himself who disciples find when they take up their cross.

Things must go, not according to your understanding but above your understanding. Submerge yourself in a lack of understanding, and I will give you my understanding. Lack of understanding is a real understanding; not knowing where you are going is really knowing where you are going. My understanding makes you without understanding. Thus Abraham went out from his homeland and did not know where he was going (Gen. 12:1). He yielded to my knowledge and abandoned his own knowledge; and by the right way he reached the right goal. Behold, that is the way of the cross. You cannot find it, but I must lead you like a blind man. Therefore not you, not a man, not a creature, but I through my Spirit and the Word, will teach you the way you must go. You must not follow the work which you choose, not the suffering which you devise, but that which comes to you against your choice, thoughts, and desires. There I call; there you must be a pupil; there it is the time; there your Master has come.[3]

Dietrich Bonhoeffer (1906–1945) was a German Lutheran pastor, theologian, and participant in the German Resistance movement against Nazism and was involved in plots to assassinate Adolf Hitler. Bonhoeffer was arrested in March 1943, imprisoned, and eventually executed by hanging shortly before the war's end.

Scripture references are from *The New Revised Standard Version*.

9

No Sorrow
Like Jesus' Sorrow

JOHN NEWTON

He had no form or majesty that we should look at him,
and no beauty that we should desire him.
He was despised and rejected by men;
a man of sorrows, and acquainted with grief;
and as one from whom men hide their faces
he was despised, and we esteemed him not.
Surely he has borne our griefs
and carried our sorrows;
yet we esteemed him stricken,
smitten by God, and afflicted. *Isaiah 53:2–4*

"Is it nothing to you, all ye that pass by? Behold and see if there be any sorrow like unto my sorrow!" It is a pathetic exclamation, by which the prophet Jeremiah expresses his grief, or rather the grief of Jerusalem, when the sins of the people had given success to the Chaldean army, and the temple and the city were destroyed. Jerusalem is poetically considered as a woman, lately reigning a queen among the nations, but now a captive, dishonoured, spoiled, and sitting upon the ground. She entreats the commiseration of those who pass by, and asks if there be any sorrow like unto her sorrow?

Such a question has often been in the heart and in the mouth of the afflicted, especially in an hour of impatience. We are all, in our turns, disposed to think our own trials peculiarly heavy, and our own cases singular. But to them who ask this question we may answer, Yes—there has been a sorrow greater than yours. They who have heard of the sorrows of Jesus, will surely, upon the hearing of Jeremiah's question, be reminded of Jesus, whether it was the intention of the prophet to personate him or not. If we conceive of him hanging upon the cross, and speaking in this language to us, "Was ever any sorrow like my sorrow?" must not we reply with admiration and gratitude, "No, Lord, never was love, never was grief, like thine."

The highest wonder ever exhibited to the world, to angels, and men, is the Son of God suffering and dying for sinners. His sufferings were indeed temporary, limited in their duration, but otherwise extreme. Witness the effects, his heaviness unto death, his consternation, his bloody sweat, his eclipse upon the cross, when deprived of what presence, which was his only, and his exceeding joy. On these accounts, no sorrow was like unto his sorrow!

The highest wonder ever exhibited to the world, to angels, and men, is the Son of God suffering and dying for sinners.

The unknown sorrows of the Redeemer are a continual source of support and consolation to his believing people. In his sufferings they contemplate his atonement, his love, and his example, and they are animated by the bright and glorious issue. For he passed from death to life, from suffering to glory.

His atonement, apprehended by faith, delivers them from guilt and condemnation, gives them peace with God, and access to him with liberty as children. Being thus delivered from their heavy burden and from the power of Satan, and having a way open for receiving supplies of grace and strength, according to their day, they are prepared to take up their cross, and to follow him.

His love, in submitting to such sorrows for their sakes, attaches their hearts to him. Great is the power of love! It makes hard things easy, and bitter, sweet. Some of us can tell, or rather we cannot easily tell, how much we would cheerfully do, or bear, or forbear, for the sake of the person whom we dearly love. But this noblest principle of the soul never can exert itself with its full strength, till it is supremely fixed upon its proper object. The love of Christ has a constraining force indeed! It is stronger than death. It overcomes the world. And "we thus love him, because he first loved us; because he loved us and gave himself for us."

His example. The thought that he suffered for them, arms them with the like mind. They look to him and are enlightened. By his cross they are crucified to the world, and the world to them. They no longer court its favor, nor are afraid of its frown. They know what they must expect, if they will be his servants, by the treatment he met with; and they are content. He who endured the contradiction of sinners against himself for them, is worthy that they should suffer likewise for him. It is their desire, neither to provoke the opposition of men, nor to dread it. They commit themselves to him, and are sure that he will not expose them to such sufferings as he endured for them. So, likewise, under all the trials and afflictions which they endure more immediately from the hand of the Lord, a lively thought of his sorrows reconciles them to their own. Thus by his stripes they are healed, and are comforted by having fellowship with him in his sufferings.

Lastly, if more were necessary (and sometimes, through remaining infirmity and surrounding temptation, every consideration is no more than necessary), they know that their Lord passed through sufferings to glory. And they know (for they have his own gracious promise), "that if they suffer with him, they shall also reign with him." They are sure, "that the sufferings of the present life are not worthy to be compared with the joy which will then be revealed; and that when Christ, who is their life, shall appear, they also shall appear with him in glory" (Col. 3:4) and therefore they are comforted in all their tribulation, and can say, "None of these things move me, neither count I my life dear unto myself, so that I may finish my course with joy" (Acts 20:24).

Excerpted from "No Sorrow Like Messiah's Sorrow" from *The Works of the Rev. John Newton*, first published by Hamilton, Adams & Co, London, 1820.

John Newton (1725–1807) was an English clergyman and former slave-ship captain. He was the author of many hymns, including "Amazing Grace."

Scripture quotations are from the *King James Version* of the Bible.

Part Two

GOD'S PURPOSE IN SUFFERING

10

The God We Had We Lose

ABRAHAM KUYPER

"I had heard of you by the hearing of the ear,
but now my eye sees you." *Job 42:5*

A woman was happy; hers was a pure delight in the possession of husband and child. An overwhelming sense of happiness found frequent expression in thanksgiving and praise. The love of her Father in heaven was so great. He made her so happy, her cup was full to overflowing. But things change. Serious illness breaks up the quiet and peace, and the child is snatched away by death. Now everything is gone. Now she cannot be comforted. Now her deeply wounded soul rises up in rebellion against God.

It has been self-deception/misleading. No, God cannot be love. How could a God who is Love be so cruel as to cast her down from the heights of her grief? And in the bewilderment of affliction, words of despair and of defiant unbelief flow from her lips. "Talk no more of God to me. Cruelty cannot love. There is no God." So the break of happiness in life becomes the break of faith in the soul. She fancied that she knew God, and now that he appears different from what she had imagined, she gives up all faith. With her child she also lost her God. And what is left in the soul is but a burned-out hearth from which the last spark has been extinguished.

This makes you feel how hard the lesson is which, through the school of suffering, must make us increase in the knowledge of God. When for the first time in our life the cross with its full weight is laid upon our shoulders, the first effect is that it makes us numb and dazed and causes all knowledge of God to be lost.

↶ The school of suffering must make us increase in the knowledge of God.

The psalm of love was so beautiful, it glided into our soul so sweetly. A God who is only Love, love for us, in order to bless us, to make our life rich and glad? Oh, who would not willingly attain unto the knowledge of such a God?

In our life among men it is indeed glorious when love and nothing but love is shown us. And how rich, then, our heart feels in the possession of a God who causes only love, only streams of happiness and peace to flow out after us.

But now dawns the day of adversity, the day of trouble and disappointment, the day of sickness and grief. "Where now is the love of God? He did not spare my dying child or come to the aid of my prayer. My child has been torn from my heart, to be carried out to the grave."

And of course, in the end, this must bring it about, that we attain to another, a better knowledge of God, which explains his dealings with us. But at first what our heart feels is that we cannot square this with our God as we imagined him, as we had dreamed him to be. The God we had, we lose, and then it costs so much bitter conflict of soul, before refined and purified in our knowledge of God, we grasp another, and now the only true God in the place thereof.

The first lesson consists in this, that in actual life, with our whole outward and inner existence, we give in to a higher decree, and bow before an All-power, against which we can do nothing. And this seems dreadful, but yet this very thing is the discovery of God as *God* in the reality of our experience.

As long as we have only just started on the way to the cross, we fancy ourselves the main object at stake; it is our happiness, our honor, our future—and God added in. According to our idea we are the center of things, and God is there to make us happy. The Father is for the sake of the child. And God's confessed Almightiness is solely and alone to serve *our* interest. This is an idea of God which is false through and through, which turns the order around and, taken in its real sense, makes self God, and God our servant.

According to our idea we are the center
of things, and God is there to
make us happy.

From this false knowledge of God the cross removes all foundation. Cast down by your sorrow and grief, you become suddenly aware that this great God does not measure nor direct the course of things according to your desire; that in his plan there are other motives that operate entirely outside of your preferences. Then you must submit, you must bend. You stand before it in utter impotence, and from this selfsame heaven, in which thus far you saw nothing but the play of light and clouds, darkness now enters into your soul, the clap of thunder reverberates in your heart, and the flaming bolt of lightning fills you with dismay.

This is the discovery of God's reality, of his Majesty which utterly overwhelms you, of an Almightiness which absorbs within itself you and everything you call yours. And for the first time you feel what it is to confront the living God. Now you know him!

And then begins the new endeavor of the soul, to learn to understand this real God. Then begins the questioning, the guessing, the pondering, *why* this Almighty God should be the way he is and do the things he does. Then the troubled heart seeks this in the after-effects of the past. It seeks this in the purpose for which the cross was laid upon us, and in the fruit which it shall bear in the unraveling of eternity. For a long time it still remains the endeavor of finding the explanation of God's doing solely and alone *in ourselves.*

Then the soul makes a still further advance. It abandons the theory of Job's friends and, like Job, receives the answer from God himself out of the whirlwind. It now learns to understand how God's appointment covers all suns and stars, all hours and centuries, and causes all creatures to revolve themselves around him, the Eternal One, as the one and only center; and, therefore, his council and plan are as high as heaven and consequently exceeded our comprehension. It learns that, not the verification of his council, but entering into the life of it, whether it be through joy, whether it be through sorrow, is our honor and the self-exaltation of our soul.

This breaks the passiveness that destroys our strength, and quickens again that which imparts heroic courage to drink the cup, to drink it willingly, and not let it be forced upon us. To will to drink, as Jesus willed to die on Golgotha—with a broken heart, to cooperate in God's work, and in this suffering cooperation with God, who slays us, to find eternal life.

The soul is thus like the sentinel who lets himself be shot down at his post and, in dying, enjoys the approving look of his general. And he rejoices therein, because he knows, and now sees, that the general, who ordered him to death, yet loved him.

Excerpted from *To Be Near Unto God* by Abraham Kuyper in 1908, translated by J. H. De Vries (New York: Macmillan, 1918).

Abraham Kuyper (1837–1920) was a Dutch politician, journalist, statesman, and theologian. He founded the Anti-Revolutionary Party and was prime minister of the Netherlands between 1901 and 1905.

11

When Cost Becomes Privilege

HELEN ROSEVEARE

He made my mouth like a sharp sword;
in the shadow of his hand he hid me;
he made me a polished arrow;
in his quiver he hid me away.
And he said to me, "You are my servant,
Israel, in whom I will be glorified." *Isaiah 49:2–3*

The night the rebel soldiers first took me captive I was beaten, flung on the ground, kicked—teeth broken, mouth and nose gashed, ribs bruised—driven at gunpoint back to my home, jeered at, insulted, threatened. I knew that if the rebel lieutenant did not pull the trigger of his revolver and end the situation, worse pain and humiliation lay ahead. It was a very dark night. I felt unutterably alone. For a brief moment, I felt God had failed me. He could have stepped in and prevented this rising crescendo of wickedness and cruelty. He could have saved me out of their hands. Why didn't he speak? Why didn't he intervene? And in desperation, I almost cried out against him: "It is too much to pay!"

Yet his love for me cost him his life. He gave himself, in that one all-sufficient atoning sacrifice at Calvary. He so loved that he gave all. His sacrifice was the expression of his great love.

But his sacrifice had achieved something. He had saved lost mankind from their sins. What was I achieving by suffering brutality at the hands of rebel soldiers? If I died (which seemed probable and imminent) no one would even know of the suffering. What was being gained? *God, why, why?*

In the dark loneliness, he met with me. He was right there, a great, wonderful, almighty God. His love enveloped me. Suddenly the "Why?" dropped away from me, and an unbelievable peace flowed in, even in the midst of the wickedness. And he breathed a word into my troubled mind: the word *privilege.*

"These are not your sufferings; they are not beating you. These are my sufferings: all I ask of you is the loan of your body."

He offered me the inestimable privilege of
sharing with him in the fellowship
of his sufferings. And it was all privilege.

For twenty years, anything I had needed I had asked of God and he had provided. Now, this night, the Almighty had stooped to ask of *me* something that he condescended to appear to need, and he offered me the *privilege* of responding. He wanted my body, in which to live, and through which to love these very rebel soldiers in the height of their wickedness. It was inconceivable, yet true. He offered me the inestimable privilege of sharing with him in some little measure, at least, in the edge of the fellowship of his sufferings. And it was all privilege.

For that night, cost became swallowed up in privilege.

What is cost, anyway? At best it is only a relative term; with no absolute value. It can be understood only in reference to the object desired, and its value may change according to circumstances. A sack of rice for about twenty dollars would seem dear in normal conditions, but the cost would be immaterial in conditions of starvation.

Early on in my missionary life in Africa, God taught me a lesson as to the meaning of *cost* in relation to what he wanted to do in my life to make me more like the Lord Jesus Christ. The palm trees in our village of Nebobongo were being stripped of leaves by an invasion of small, brightly coloured weaver birds, and this was affecting the yield of urgently needed oil from the palm nuts, a basic commodity in both our local diet and also the local industrial economy.

I offered the children of the village a penny for every bird shot. From then on, we noticed apparently wanton destruction of the lower boughs of flowering acacia trees, of red-leaved poinsettia shrubs, of blossom-bearing branches of coffee bushes, of fruit-laden branches of orange and grapefruit trees.

Everywhere we found children whittling away at branches from any accessible tree or bush, using any available weapon as a knife, to create arrows. Even in the back row of the classroom, during a math lesson, I heard the inescapable telltale sound of sandpapering, as a banana leaf was rubbed energetically up and down a stripped stem to polish an amazingly straight arrow shaft for the all-important, new, financially fruitful hobby of archery!

We had to weigh up the comparative "costs." We needed oranges and grapefruit in our diet, so those trees became banned to the amateur archers. We sold coffee beans to augment our hospital funds, so those bushes were forbidden. But we decided the beauty afforded by the bright yellow blossoms and feathery green leaves of the acacia trees was only appreciated by the white foreigners. The branches were not even of value for firewood. The "cost" as measured by the acacia trees was decidedly less than that caused by the loss of the palm leaves through the destruction by the weaver birds. From then on, bright yellow acacia blossoms and feathery green leaves could be found littered all over the paths of the village, the price paid for the construction of arrows to destroy the destructive birds.

So the Lord spoke directly to me about what he wanted to do in my life. I had liked the bright yellow acacia trees. They broke up, for me, the monotony of green that shrouds the great rain forests. But we needed the palm oil. The one was relinquished for the other. The bright flowers and leaves were sacrificed to make the needed arrows. There was nothing wrong with the flowers and leaves. In fact, they were essential for the life and reproduction of the trees. Yet they were not only unnecessary, they were definitely a hindrance for an arrow. The side branches, thorns, and knots needed smoothing off. It seemed that each branch became impersonalized, losing its own particular form and beauty, sacrificed for the one aim of producing a straight, well-balanced arrow. Even the bark had to be stripped off, leaving the stem naked, exposed to the wind and rain. The branch as such had been destroyed. It could no longer feed or reproduce: its beauty had been vandalized. It could no longer be recognized for itself; and even its power to survive in all weathers would be challenged.

This wanton act of destruction might seem a senseless waste of God-given beauty. Yet if from the destructive process, the polished shaft of the arrow that emerged was able to rid the community of hordes of preying birds, preserving for us an essential source of health-producing food, would not the "cost" seem more acceptable?

Could I see that God wanted to transform my life from a somewhat ugly, useless branch to an arrow, a tool usable in his hands, for the furtherance of his purposes? It was said of the Lord Jesus Christ: "Before I was born the LORD called me; from my birth he has made mention of my name. He made my mouth like a sharpened sword, in the shadow of his hand he hid me; he made me into a polished arrow and concealed me in his quiver. He said to me, 'You are my servant, Israel, in whom I will display my splendor'" (Isa. 49:1–3).

God wanted to transform my life from a somewhat ugly, useless branch to an arrow, a tool usable in his hands, for the furtherance of his purposes.

To be thus transformed, was I willing—am I still willing—for the whittling, sandpapering, stripping processes necessary in my Christian life? The ruthless pulling off of leaves and flowers might include doing without a television set or washing machine, remaining single in order to see a job done, reevaluating the worthiness of the ambition to be a "good" doctor (according to *my* terms and values). The snapping off of thorns might include drastic dealing with hidden jealousies and unknown prides, giving up prized rights in leadership and administration. The final stripping of the bark might include lessons to be learned regarding death to self—self-defense, self-pity, self-justification, self-vindication, self-sufficiency, all the mechanisms of preventing the hurt of too-deep involvement. Am I prepared for the pain, which may at times seem like sacrifice, in order to be made into a tool in his service? My willingness will be a measure of the sincerity of my desire to express my heartfelt gratitude to him for his so-great salvation.

To love the Lord my God with *all* my soul will involve a spiritual cost. I'll have to give him my heart, and let him love through it whom and how he wills, even if this seems at times to break my heart.

To love the Lord my God with *all* my soul will involve a volitional and emotional cost. I'll have to give him my will, my rights to decide and choose, and all my relationships, for him to guide and control, even when I cannot understand his reasoning.

To love the Lord my God with *all* my mind will involve an intellectual cost. I must give him my mind, my intelligence, my reasoning powers, and trust him to work through them, even when he may appear to act in contradiction to common sense.

To love the Lord my God with *all* my strength will involve a physical cost. I must give him my body to indwell, and through which to speak, whether he chooses by health or sickness, by strength or weakness, and trust him utterly with the outcome.

The sum of these apparent costs (as with the stripping of the branch to create the arrow) could be considered as the sacrifice that I am invited to offer him as the response of my whole being to his love for me in that one "full, perfect, and sufficient sacrifice, oblation, and satisfaction for the sins of the whole world." It is my way of expressing my gratitude to Christ for all he is, and for all he has done and given for me.

Excerpted from *Living Sacrifice: Willing to Be Whittled as an Arrow* by Helen Roseveare, © 2007 Christian Focus Publications. Used by permission.

Dr. Helen Roseveare served as a medical missionary to the Congo from 1953 to 1973. In 1964 she was taken prisoner of rebel forces and remained prisoner for five months, during which she was beaten and raped. She is now retired and lives in Northern Ireland. Her life of service was portrayed in the 1989 film *Mama Luka Comes Home*.

Scripture references are from *The Holy Bible: New International Version.*®

12

Prepared for Usefulness

A. W. TOZER

"I will put this third into the fire,
and refine them as one refines silver,
and test them as gold is tested.
They will call upon my name,
and I will answer them.
I will say, 'They are my people';
and they will say, 'The LORD is my God.'"
Zechariah 13:9

It was the enraptured Samuel Rutherford who could shout in the midst of serious and painful trials, "Praise God for the hammer, the file, and the furnace."

The hammer is a useful tool, but the nail, if it had feeling and intelligence could present another side of the story. For the nail knows the hammer only as an opponent, a brutal, merciless enemy who lives to pound it into submission. To beat it down out of sight and clinch it into place. That is the nail's view of the hammer, and it is accurate except for one thing: The nail forgets that both it and the hammer are servants of the same workman. Let the nail but remember that the hammer is held by the workman and all resentment toward it will disappear. The carpenter decides whose head shall be beaten next and what hammer shall be used in the beating. That is his sovereign right. When the nail has surrendered to the will of the workman and has gotten a little glimpse of his benign plans for its future, it will yield to the hammer without complaint.

The file is more painful still, for its business is to bite into the soft metal, scraping and eating away the edges till it has shaped the metal to its will. Yet the file has, in truth, no real will in the matter, but serves another master as the metal also does. It is the master and not the file that decides how much shall be eaten away, what shape the metal shall take and how long the painful filing shall continue. Let the metal accept the will of the master and it will not try to dictate when or how it shall be filed.

As for the furnace, it is the worst of all. Ruthless and savage, it leaps at every combustible thing that enters it and never relaxes its fury till it has reduced it all to shapeless ashes. All that refuses to burn is melted to a mass of helpless matter, without will or purpose of its own. When everything is melted that will melt and all is burned that will burn, then and not till then the furnace calms down and rests from its destructive fury.

With all this known to him, how could Rutherford find it in his heart to praise God for the hammer, the file, and the furnace? The answer is simply that he loved the Master of the hammer, he adored the Workman who wielded the file, he worshiped the Lord who heated the furnace for the everlasting blessing of his children. He had felt the hammer till its rough beatings no longer hurt; he had endured the file till he had come actually to enjoy its biting; he had walked with God in the furnace so long that it had become as his natural habitat. That does not overstate the facts. His letters reveal as much.

Such doctrine as this does not find much sympathy among Christians in these soft and carnal days. We tend to think of

Christianity as a painless system by which we can escape the penalty of past sins and attain to heaven at last. The flaming desire to be rid of every unholy thing and to put on the likeness of Christ at any cost is not often found among us. We expect to enter the everlasting kingdom of our Father and to sit down around the table with sages, saints and martyrs; and through the grace of God, maybe we shall; yes maybe we shall. But for the most of us it could prove at first an embarrassing experience. Ours might be the silence of the untried soldier in the presence of the battle-hardened heroes who have fought the fight and won the victory and who have scars to prove that they were present when the battle was joined.

The devil, things, and people being what they are, it is necessary for God to use the hammer, the file, and the furnace in his holy work of preparing a saint for true sainthood. It is doubtful whether God can bless a man greatly until he has hurt him deeply.

It is doubtful whether God can bless
a man greatly until he has hurt him deeply.

Without doubt we of this generation have become too soft to scale great spiritual heights. Salvation has come to mean deliverance from unpleasant things. Our hymns and sermons create for us a religion of consolations and pleasantness. We overlook the place of the thorns, the cross, and the blood. We ignore the function of the hammer and the file.

Strange as it may sound, it is yet true that much of the suffering we are called upon to endure on the highway of holiness is an inward suffering for which scarcely an external cause can be found. For our journey is an inward journey, and our real foes are invisible to the eyes of men. Attacks of darkness, of despondency, of acute self-depreciation may be endured without any change in our outward circumstances. Only the enemy and God and the hard-pressed Christian know what has taken place. The inward suffering has been great and a mighty work of purification has been accomplished, but the heart knoweth its own sorrow and no one else can share it. God has cleansed his child in the only way he can, circumstance being what they are. Thank God for the furnace.

Excerpted from "Praise God for the Furnace," a chapter in *The Root of the Righteous: Tapping the Bedrock of True Spirituality* by A. W. Tozer, copyright © 1955, 1983 by Lowell Tozer. Used by permission of WingSpread Publishers, a division of Zur Ltd., 800-884-4571.

Aiden Wilson Tozer (1897–1963) was a Christian and Missionary Alliance pastor, preacher, author, magazine editor, Bible conference speaker, and spiritual mentor.

13

The Test of a Crisis

MARTYN LLOYD-JONES

And when the flame went up toward heaven from
the altar, the angel of the LORD went up in the flame
of the altar. Now Manoah and his wife were watching,
and they fell on their faces to the ground. . . .

Then Manoah knew that he was the angel of the LORD.
And Manoah said to his wife, "We shall surely die,
for we have seen God." But his wife said to him,
"If the LORD had meant to kill us, he would not have
accepted a burnt offering and a grain offering at our
hands, or shown us all these things, or now announced
to us such things as these." *Judges 13:20, 22–23*

These words are the simple yet profound record of how the father
and mother of Samson reacted to the same set of difficult and critical
circumstances in which they suddenly found themselves. You can
read the whole of the chapter prior to these verses and still not really
know Manoah and his wife. But here, in these two verses, suddenly
and in a flash, we see them as they are.

Likewise, when we go through a crisis, it shows exactly and
precisely what kind of person we really are. In times when life is

pursuing the ordinary tenor of its way, we all succeed in making a fair show. It is so easy to live an artificial and a superficial life and to persuade ourselves that we really are what we would like to be. But in a time of trial and of crisis, the natural, the real, and true come into view.

A time of crisis and of difficulty also tests and demonstrates very clearly what we really believe, and the nature of our religious faith. For, after all, merely to see the greatness of Samson's mother as a woman, and as a strong character, is to miss what is really significant in the story. The striking thing is the faith, the insight, the understanding, the firm grasp of religion, which really made her what she was, and which enabled her to shame her husband and to reproach him for his weakness and his fear.

A time of crisis and of difficulty also tests and demonstrates very clearly what we really believe.

There is nothing which is quite so sad and so tragic in the life and experience of a minister as to find people whose religion does not seem to give them anything, or to be of the slightest value to them face to face with the greatest needs and crises of life such as illness, bereavement and sorrow, disaster or threatened calamity, or a war. They had appeared to be such excellent examples of religious people. They had never been guilty of any heretical statement or of any gross violation of the moral code. They seemed in times of normality to be the ideal type of religious person. And yet, when their religion was put to the test and was needed most of all, it suddenly seemed to mean nothing and to be quite useless.

There are others whose interest in religion has been their main intellectual hobby. Religion was something to talk about and to argue about, something which a man could take up and put down. It had never become a part of their inner actual experience. It had never become a part of them and of their lives. Here again, in the crisis, all the knowledge and the interest seem to be useless and valueless.

The classic example of this is John Wesley prior to his conversion. He, in a sense, knew all about religion, but while crossing the Atlantic, and in a terrible storm, which seemed to be leading to certain death, he felt that he had nothing. He was afraid to die and afraid of everything. And what struck him was the contrast presented by the Moravian Brethren who were on the same ship. They were, in comparison with Wesley, ignorant men, but their religion meant something real and vital to them. It held them in the storm, and gave them peace and calmness, and indeed joy, even face to face with death. Wesley's religion appeared to be excellent. He gave all his goods to the poor, he preached in prisons, and he had crossed that Atlantic to preach to pagans in Georgia. He was a man of immense knowledge of things religious. And yet the trial revealed to him and to others the nature of his religion, and showed it to be worthless.

A time of crisis, then, tests us, and our religion, even as it tested Manoah and his wife. The tragedy is that so many of us resemble the former rather than the latter. We are anxious to be blessed, and we look to religion for all the gifts and blessing that it has to give. Like Manoah we may be fervent in our prayers and, judged by actions and our external appearance, we may appear and, indeed, actually be, highly devout persons. While all goes well, and while our prayers are answered and all our desires appear to be gratified, we are full of praise and of thanksgiving, even as Manoah was when his request was granted. But, then, suddenly, everything seems to go wrong. The situation is perplexing and baffling and quite the contrary of what we had expected and anticipated. Now, far too often, we behave as Manoah did. We seem to break down altogether and to lose hope entirely. We jump to conclusions, and almost invariably, to the worst conclusion that is possible in the given circumstances, the same assumption as that which led Manoah to his worst conclusion, (namely) that somehow or other, God is against us, and that all we had so fondly imagined to be an expression of God's goodness and kindness was nothing but an illusion.

We need not behave as Manoah did. His wife shows us clearly how all that is to be avoided. She behaved as we should all behave. She did what we should all do in like circumstances. Seeing and observing her husband's collapse, his fear and his whimpering, and listening to his foreboding of evil and his dark prophecies and his doubtings of the goodness of God, she doesn't cry or shout, she doesn't give way to hysteria and collapse in a state of unconsciousness, she doesn't ask irreverent questions or utter complaints against God—she thinks, she reasons, she ponders the matter, and with magnificent logic she arrives at the only conclusion that is really valid.

In the midst of disaster and trying difficulties,
the Christian religion, instead of acting like
a charm or a drug, asks us to think and
to employ logic.

In the midst of disaster and trying difficulties, the Christian religion, instead of acting like a charm or a drug, and doing everything for us, and suddenly putting everything right, asks us, nay rather commands us, to think and to employ logic.

Her conclusions are as valid today as when she uttered them. She simply stated what she reasoned about God in her own way, and in her own language, and in the context of the events which confronted her and her husband.

The first principle she stated is that *God is never capricious*. "If the Lord were pleased to kill us," argues the woman, "he would not have received a burnt offering and a meat offering at our hands." It appeared at the moment as if God were suddenly going to reverse everything that he had just been doing. Having smiled upon these people, it looked as if without any apparent cause or reason he was now frowning upon them, and on the point of destroying them. Circumstances often seem to give us that impression. Everything suddenly seems to go wrong and to be working in the reverse direction, and the suggestion comes to us that God is not really interested in us, and not concerned about us.

Now, of one thing we can always be absolutely certain—God is not like that. By his very nature and being there is nothing more glorious than the eternal constancy of God. He is "the father of light with whom is no variableness neither shadow of turning." He does not say one thing and then do the opposite. He does not play with us and mock us. He is never capricious.

Secondly, *God is never unjust in his dealings with us*. Samson's mother argues very rightly, that for God to have led her and her husband to do certain things merely in order that he might punish and destroy them for so doing, would be an act of sheer injustice. And that is something she knows to be utterly unthinkable where God is concerned.

It is not that she understands exactly and precisely what is happening to them, or as to what is the exact meaning of the events they are witnessing. But whatever their meaning may be, of this she is certain, that God is never unjust or unrighteous. Seeing, as we do, but one aspect or one angle or phase of a problem or a situation, we often fail to see the righteousness or the justice of events. But that is entirely due to our restricted field of vision. Furthermore, our minds are warped, and we are tarnished and perverted by sin. Our very ideas of rightness are not true. Our selfishness blurs our vision and poisons our understanding. We do not even know what is ultimately the best for ourselves, there is so much darkness mixed with our light.

The third principle is that *God never contradicts himself and his own gracious purposes.* Listen to this woman's superb logic. "If the Lord were pleased to kill us . . . he would not have shewed us all these things nor would as at this time have told us such things as these." In effect, she turned to her husband and said, *Is it conceivable that the God who has just given us such striking tokens of his presence and his goodness is now going to destroy us? Nay, more, is it conceivable that the One who has intervened in our lives, and has come to us to tell us that he has certain plans in store for us and certain purposes which he proposes to bring to pass in us and through us, is it conceivable that having initiated all this he is now suddenly going to end it all? I do not pretend to understand, but to me, it is unthinkable that God should start a process and then suddenly reverse it or destroy it.*

We have in her words what St. Paul states so frequently and so eloquently. "Being confident of this very thing, that he which hath begun a good work in you will perform it until the day of Jesus Christ." But the argument is still stronger, "He that spared not his own Son but delivered him up for us all, how shall he not with him also freely give us all things?" Is God who has already done the greater, yea, the greatest thing of all, likely to fail us in the lesser? Is the love of God, which is so great as to send his only-begotten Son to that cruel death on Calvary's Hill, likely to forsake you, having done that?

You may not understand what is happening to you; it may seem, to you, all wrong. Trust yourself to him. Believe when you cannot prove. Hold on to his constancy, his justice, his eternal purposes for you in Christ. Regard these as absolutes, which can never be shaken, build your case logically upon them, remain steadfast and unshaken, confident that ultimately all will be made plain and all will be well.

Adapted from *Why Does God Allow Suffering?* ©1994 Elizabeth Catherwood. Published by Crossway Books.

David Martyn Lloyd-Jones (1899–1981) was minister of Westminster Chapel in London for thirty years.

14

Too Good to Suffer?

ST. AUGUSTINE

"For he makes his sun rise on the evil and on the good,
and sends rain on the just and on the unjust." *Matthew 5:45*

The patience of God invites the wicked to repentance, even as the scourge of God educates the good to patience. So, too, does the mercy of God embrace the good that it may cherish them, as the severity of God arrests the wicked to punish them. To the divine providence it has seemed good to prepare in the world to come for the righteous good things, which the unrighteous shall not enjoy; and for the wicked evil things, by which the good shall not be tormented. But as for the good things of this life, and its ills, God has willed that these should be common to both; that we might not too eagerly covet the things which wicked men are seen equally to enjoy, nor shrink with an unseemly fear from the ills which even good men often suffer.

There is, too, a very great difference in the purpose served both by those events which we call adverse and those called prosperous. For the good man is neither uplifted with the good things of time, nor broken by its ills; but the wicked man, because he is corrupted by this world's happiness, feels himself punished by its unhappiness.

Yet often, even in the present distribution of temporal things, does God plainly evince his own interference. For if every sin were now visited with manifest punishment, nothing would seem to be reserved for the final judgment; on the other hand, if no sin received now a plainly divine punishment, it would be concluded that there is no divine providence at all. And so of the good things of this life: if God did not by a very visible liberality confer these on some of those persons who ask for them, we should say that these good things were not at his disposal; and if he gave them to all who sought them, we should suppose that such were the only rewards of his service; and such a service would make us not godly, but greedy rather, and covetous.

Wherefore, though good and bad men suffer alike, we must not suppose that there is no difference between the men themselves, because there is no difference in what they both suffer. For even in the likeness of the sufferings, there remains an unlikeness in the sufferers; and though exposed to the same anguish, virtue and vice are not the same thing. For as the same fire causes gold to glow brightly, and chaff to smoke; and under the same flail the straw is beaten small, while the grain is cleansed; and as the lees are not mixed with the oil, though squeezed out of the vat by the same pressure, so the same violence of affliction proves, purges, clarifies the good, but damns, ruins, exterminates the wicked. And thus it is that in the same affliction the wicked detest God and blaspheme, while the good pray and praise. So material a difference does it make, not what ills are suffered, but what kind of man suffers them. For, stirred up with the same movement, mud exhales a horrible stench, and ointment emits a fragrant odor.

What, then, have the Christians suffered, which would not profit every one who duly and faithfully considered the following circumstances? First of all, they must humbly consider those very sins which have provoked God to fill the world with such terrible disasters; for although they be far from the excesses of wicked, immoral, and ungodly men, yet they do not judge themselves so clean removed from all faults as to be too good to suffer for these even temporal ills. For every man, however laudably he lives, yet yields in some points to the lust of the flesh. Though he do not fall into gross enormity of wickedness, and abandoned viciousness, and abominable profanity, yet he slips into some sins, either rarely or so much the more frequently as the sins seem of less account.

The same violence of affliction proves, purges, clarifies the good, but damns, ruins, exterminates the wicked.

Where can we readily find a man who holds in fit and just estimation those persons on account of whose revolting pride, luxury, and avarice, and cursed iniquities and impiety, God now smites the earth as his predictions threatened? Where is the man who lives with them in the style in which it becomes us to live with them? For often we wickedly blind ourselves to the occasions of teaching and admonishing them, sometimes even of reprimanding and chiding them, either because we shrink from the labor or are ashamed to offend them, or because we fear to lose good friendships, lest this should stand in the way of our advancement, or injure us in some worldly matter, which either our covetous disposition desires to obtain, or our weakness shrinks from losing. So that, although the conduct of wicked men is distasteful to the good, and therefore they do not fall with them into that damnation which in the next life awaits such persons, yet, because they spare their damnable sins through fear, therefore, even though their own sins be slight and venial, they are justly scourged with the wicked in this world, though in eternity they quite escape punishment. Justly, when God afflicts them in common with the wicked, do they find this life bitter, through love of whose sweetness they declined to be bitter to these sinners.

Why are the good chastised along with the wicked, when God is pleased to visit with temporal punishments the profligate manners of a community? They are punished together, not because they have spent an equally corrupt life, but because the good as well as the wicked, though not equally with them, love this present life; while they ought to hold it cheap, that the wicked, being admonished and reformed by their example, might lay hold of life eternal. And if they will not be the companions of the good in seeking life everlasting, they should be loved as enemies, and be dealt with patiently. For so long as they live, it remains uncertain whether they may not come to a better mind.

There is another reason why the good are afflicted with temporal calamities—the reason which Job's case exemplifies: that the human spirit may be proved, and that it may be manifested with what fortitude of pious trust, and with how unmercenary a love, it cleaves to God.

Adapted from *The City of God* by St. Augustine.

Augustine of Hippo (354–430) was a philosopher and theologian.

15

Faith Tried and Proved

CHARLES HADDON SPURGEON

In this you rejoice, though now for a little while,
if necessary, you have been grieved by various trials,
so that the tested genuineness of your faith—more
precious than gold that perishes though it is tested
by fire may be found to result in praise and glory
and honor at the revelation of Jesus Christ. *1 Peter 1:6–7*

There is an invaluable blessing which is gained by the trial of our faith. The blessing gained is this, that our faith is tried and proved. The way of trying whether you are a good soldier is to go down to the battle. The way to try whether a ship is well built is, not merely to order the surveyor to examine her, but to send her to sea: a storm will be the best test of her staunchness.

We need trials as a test as much as we need divine truth as our food. Admire the ancient types placed in the ark of the covenant of old: two things were laid close together—the pot of manna and the rod. See how heavenly food and heavenly rule go together: how our sustenance and our chastening are equally provided for! A Christian cannot live without the manna nor without the rod. The two must go together. I mean this, that it is as great a mercy to have your salvation proved to you under trial as it is to have it sustained in you by the consolations of the Spirit of God. Sanctified tribulations work the proof of our faith, and this is more precious than that of gold which perisheth, though it be tried by fire.

It is as great a mercy to have your salvation proved to you under trial as it is to have it sustained in you by the consolations of the Spirit of God.

Now, when we are able to bear it without starting aside, the trial proves our sincerity. Coming out of a trouble the Christian says to himself, "Yes, I held fast mine integrity, and did not let it go. Blessed be God, I was not afraid of threatening; I was not crushed by losses; I was kept true to God under pressure. Now, I am sure that my religion is not a mere profession, but a real consecration to God. It has endured the fire, being kept by the power of God."

Next, it proves the truthfulness of our doctrinal belief. Oh, yes, you may say, "I have heard Mr. Spurgeon expound the doctrines, and I have believed them." This is poor work; but if you have been sick, and found a comfort in those doctrines, then you are assured of their truth. If you have been on the borders of the grave, and the gospel has given you joy and gladness, then you know how true it is. Experimental knowledge is the best and surest. If you have seen others pass through death itself triumphantly you have said, "This is proof to me: my faith is no guess-work: I have seen for myself." Is not this assurance cheaply purchased at any price? May we not count it all joy when the Lord puts us in the way of getting it? It seems to me that doubt is worse than trial. I had sooner suffer any affliction than be left to question the gospel or my own interest in it. Certainly it is a jewel worth purchasing even with our heart's blood.

Next, your own faith in God is proved when you can cling to him under temptation. Not only your sincerity, but the divinity of your faith is proved; for a faith that is never tried, how can you depend upon it? But if in the darkest hour you have still said, "I cast my burden upon the Lord, and he will sustain me," and you find he does sustain you, then is your faith that of God's elect. If in temptation you cry to God in prayer that you may keep your garment unspotted, and he helps you to do so, then also are you sure that yours is the faith which the Spirit begets in the soul. After a great fight of affliction, when I come forth a conqueror, I know that I do believe in God, and I know that this faith makes me a partaker of covenant blessings; from this I may fairly argue that my faith is of the right kind.

I find it especially sweet to learn the great strength of the Lord in my own weakness. We find out under trial where we are most weak, and just then in answer to prayer strength is given answerable to the need. The Lord suits the help to the hindrance, and puts the plaster on the wound. In the very hour when it is needed, the needed grace is given. Does this not tend to breed assurance of faith?

In the very hour when it is needed,
the needed grace is given. Does this not
tend to breed assurance of faith?

It is a splendid thing to be able to prove even to Satan the purity of your motives. That was the great gain of Job. There was no question about his outward conduct, but the question was about his motive. "Ah," says the devil, "he serves God for what he gets out of him. Hast thou not set a hedge about him and all that he has? His is cupboard love: he cares nothing for God himself, he only cares for the reward of his virtue." Well, he is tried, and everything is taken away, and when he cries, "Though he slay me, yet will I trust in him," when he blesses the taking as well as the giving God, then the devil himself could not have the prudence to accuse him again. As to Job's own conscience, it would be quite settled and confirmed as to his pure love to God. My brethren, I reckon that the endurance of every imaginable suffering and trial would be a small price to pay for a settled assurance, which would forever prevent the possibility of doubt. Never mind the waves if they wash you upon this rock. Therefore, when you are tempted, "Count it all joy" that you are tried, because you will thus receive a proof of your love, a proof of your faith, a proof of your being the true-born children of God.

James says, "Count it." A man requires to be trained to be a good accountant; it is an art which needs to be learned. What muddles some of us would make if we had to settle accounts and manage disbursements and incomings without the aid of a clerk! How we should get entangled with balances and deficits! We could much easier spend money than count it. But when a man once knows the science of bookkeeping, and gets into the way of it, he readily arrives at the true position of affairs. He has learned to count, and no error escapes his eye. James gives us a ready reckoner, and teaches us in our troubles how to count. He sets before us a different kind of measure from that which carnal reason would use: the shekel of the sanctuary was very different from the shekel in common commerce, and so is the counting of faith far other than that of human judgment. He bids us take our pen and sit down quickly and write at his correct dictation. You are going to write down, "Manifold temptations"; that would be so much on the wrong side: but instead thereof he bids you set down the proving of your faith, and this one asset transforms the transaction into a substantial gain.

Trials are like a fire; they burn up nothing in us but the dross, and they make the gold all the purer. Put down the testing process as a clear gain, and, instead of being sorry about it, count it all joy when ye fall into divers trials, for this bestows upon you a proof of your faith.

Excerpted from "A Joy in All Trials," A Sermon (No. 1704) Delivered on Lord's Day Morning, February 4th, 1883, by C. H. Spurgeon, At the Metropolitan Tabernacle, Newington, England.

Charles Haddon Spurgeon (1834–1892) was a British Baptist minister who is still known as the "Prince of Preachers."

16

Choosing Trust

JERRY BRIDGES

In God I trust; I shall not be afraid. *Psalm 56:11*

Despite the fact that he was a warrior of great skill and courage, there were times when David was afraid. The heading of Psalm 56 indicates the occasion of David's writing: "When the Philistines had seized him in Gath." The historical narrative of that incident says that he "was very much afraid of Achish king of Gath" (1 Sam. 21:12).

But despite David's fear, he said to God, "I will trust in you . . . I will not be afraid." Repeatedly in the psalms we find the determination to trust God—choosing to trust him despite all appearances. David's declaration is Psalm 23:4, "I will fear no evil," is equivalent to "I will trust in God in the face of evil." In Psalm 16:8 he says, "I have set the LORD always before me. Because he is at my right hand, I will not be shaken." To set the Lord before me is to recognize his presence and his constant help, but this is something we must choose to do.

For many years in my own pilgrimage of seeking to come to a place of trusting God at all times—I am still far from the end of the journey—I was a prisoner to my feelings. I mistakenly thought I could not trust God unless I *felt* like trusting him (which I almost never did in times of adversity). Now I am learning that trusting

God is first of all a matter of the will, and is not dependent on my feelings. I choose to trust God and my feelings eventually follow.

I choose to trust God and my feelings eventually follow.

John Newton, author of the hymn "Amazing Grace," watched cancer slowly and painfully kill his wife over a period of many months. In recounting those days, John Newton said:

> I believe it was about two or three months before her death, when I was walking up and down the room, offering disjointed prayers from a heart torn with distress, that a thought suddenly struck me, with unusual force, to this effect—"The promises of God must be true; surely the Lord will help me, *if I am willing to be helped!*" It occurred to me, that we are often led . . . [from an undue regard of our feelings], to indulge that unprofitable grief which both our duty and our peace require us to resist to the utmost of our power. I instantly said aloud, "Lord, I am helpless indeed, in myself, but I hope I am willing, without reserve, that thou shouldest help me."[1]

John Newton was helped in a remarkable way. During those remaining months he tended to his usual duties as an Anglican minister and was able to say, "Through the whole of my painful trial, I attended all my stated and occasional services as usual; and a stranger would scarcely have discovered, either by my words or looks, that I was in trouble. [The long affliction] did not prevent me from preaching a single sermon, and I preached on the day of her death . . . I likewise preached three times while she lay dead in the house . . . And after she was deposited in the vault, I preached her funeral sermon."[2]

How was John Newton helped? First he chose to be helped.

He realized it was his duty to resist "to the utmost of our power" an inordinate amount of grief and distraction. He realized it was sinful to wallow in self-pity. Then he turned to the Lord, not even asking, but only indicating his *willingness* to be helped. Then he said, "I was not supported by lively sensible consolations, but by being enabled to realize to my mind some great and leading truths of the word of God."[3] The Spirit of God helped him by making needed truths of Scripture alive to him. He chose to trust God, he turned to God in an attitude of dependence, and he was enabled to realize certain great truths of Scripture. Choice, prayer, and the Word of God were the crucial elements of his being helped to trust God.

The same David who said in Psalm 56:4, "In God I trust; I will not be afraid" said in Psalm 34:4, "I sought the LORD, and he answered me; he delivered me from all my fears." There is no conflict between saying, "I will not be afraid" and asking God to deliver us from our fears. David recognized it was his responsibility to choose to trust God, but also that he was dependent upon the Lord for the ability to do it.

Trust is not a passive state of mind.
It is a vigorous act of the soul.

Whenever I teach on the subject of personal holiness, I always stress that we are *responsible* to obey the will of God, but we are *dependent* upon the Holy Spirit for the enabling power to do it. The same principle applies in the realm of trusting God. We are responsible to trust him in times of adversity but we are dependent upon the Holy Spirit to enable us to do so.

Trust is not a passive state of mind. It is a vigorous act of the soul by which we choose to lay hold on the promises of God and cling to them despite the adversity that at times seeks to overwhelm us.

A pitfall to trusting God, which we are prone to fall into, is to turn to God in trust in the greater crisis experiences of life while seeking to work through the minor difficulties ourselves. A disposition to trust in ourselves is part of our sinful nature. It sometimes takes a major crisis, or at least a moderate one, to turn us toward the Lord. A mark of Christian maturity is to continually trust the Lord in the minutiae of daily life. If we learn to trust God in the minor adversities, we will be better prepared to trust him in the major ones.

I once asked a dear saint of God who has experienced much adversity whether she found it as difficult to trust God in the minor difficulties of life as in the major ones. She replied that she found the minor ones more difficult. In times of major crisis she readily realized her utter dependence on God and quickly turned to him, but she often tried to work through the more ordinary adversities herself. Let us learn from her experience and seek to trust God in the ordinary circumstances of life.

But whether the difficulty is major or minor, we must choose to trust God. We must learn to say with the psalmist, "When I am afraid, I will trust in you."

Adapted from *Trusting God* ©1988 by Jerry Bridges, published by NavPress, Colorado Springs, CO. Used by permission.

Jerry Bridges has been on staff with the The Navigators since 1955.

Scripture references are from *The Holy Bible: New International Version.*

17

Dying Well

D. A CARSON

You return man to dust
and say, "Return, O children of man!"
For a thousand years in your sight
are but as yesterday when it is past,
or as a watch in tho night. . . .
For all our days pass away under your wrath;
we bring our years to an end like a sigh.
The years of our life are seventy,
or even by reason of strength eighty;
yet their span is but toil and trouble;
they are soon gone, and we fly away.
Who considers the power of your anger,
and your wrath according to the fear of you?
So teach us to number our days
that wo may yet a heart of wisdom. *Psalm 90:3–4, 9–12*

There was a time when Christians were known as people who knew how to die well. It was part of Christian concern to be known as people who know how to die well. But today, if I start talking about death everyone becomes very nervous.

Not long ago in my church, a woman I'll call Mary experienced

a recurrence of cancer. Within a few months it had spread throughout her body, and despite treatment, she was very ill. The people in
our church gathered for prayer. And although this is not a church
from a charismatic tradition, the prayers throughout the day became
more and more enthusiastic.

"Lord, you've said you will answer if two or three are in agreement. We have 287 in agreement, and we want you to heal her!"

"Jesus Christ is the same yesterday, today, and tomorrow. We
want you to show that you are still the Great Physician!"

"Lord, will you not have mercy on her husband and her
children?"

Finally it was my wife's turn to pray (she who had almost lost
her life to cancer twice) and she prayed, "Heavenly Father, we would
love it if you would heal Mary. But if it is not your will to heal her,
teach her to die well. She is going to die anyway, and so if the time
is now, teach her to die well. Give her a joy of the Lord. Give her a
heritage of godly faith, with one foot firmly planted in heaven, so
that her husband and children will be stamped by it, and will look
to Christ. We don't ask that she have an easy time, but ask that she
be so full grace, people will see Christ in her."

Well, you could have cut the air with a knife. No longer were
there 287 people agreeing in prayer. My wife's prayer seemed to create a break in the chain. She was letting down her side. We found out
afterward that some of Mary's relatives rather wished my wife would
go to heaven first so she would know whereof she was praying!

A few months later, Mary's husband called me, and was desperate to talk. Mary's health was going down and down despite
every treatment conceivable. The church was wonderful, bringing
in food, reminding them, "We're praying for you . . . the Lord
is faithful." But he wanted permission to talk about his wife's
impending death. The heated atmosphere had made it impossible

for them to talk in those terms, as if it would no longer be walking by faith. Mary couldn't focus on eternity or talk about it, because there were so many Christians around her telling her she was going to be healed.

Well-intentioned, but poorly informed brothers and sisters who try to deflect people from thinking about death, or who hold out the constant hope of healing, keep them so occupied with matters in this world that they have neither the time nor the energy to think about the next world. They succeed only in robbing their loved ones of the enormous comforts of the gospel as they step into eternity.

Whatever the church does, it should prepare its members to face death and meet God. You cannot live faithfully in this life unless you are ready for the next. You can't preserve morality or spirituality or doctrinal purity or faithfulness unless you are living in light of eternity.

One day we will stand in the presence of the King with resurrection bodies and see everything from a different angle than we can see now. We'll see everything through the triumphs of Christ—even the cancer that took us, or the persecution—all these things will look very different fifty billion years into eternity.

In September 1542, Magdalene, one of the daughters of Martin Luther, lay dying, her father weeping at her side. He asked her, "Magdalene, my dear little daughter, would you like to stay here with your father, or would you willingly go to your Father yonder?"

Magdalene answered, "Darling father, as God wills." Luther wept, holding his daughter in his arms, praying that God might free her; and she died.

As she was laid in her coffin, Martin Luther declared, "Darling Lena, you will rise and shine like a star, yea like the sun . . . I am happy in spirit, but the flesh is sorrowful and will not be content, the parting grieves me beyond measure . . . I have sent a saint to heaven."

Is not some of the pain and sorrow in this life used in God's providential hand to make us homesick for heaven, to detach us from this world, to prepare us for heaven, to draw our attention to himself, and away from the world of merely physical things?

Is not some of the pain and sorrow in this life used in God's providential hand to make us homesick for heaven?

In Psalm 90 we see that as Moses stares at death, he thinks through its relation to life, to sin, to God, and strives to understand what death means. And then he asks for wisdom to live his life in light of that death. He would have utterly scorned the modern mood that wants to live life as if death were not there waiting for us at the end. Moses wants us "to number our days," that is, to recognize the limit that is imposed on us, and to live with that limit in full view. Only in this way can we "gain a heart of wisdom."

Now let us suppose that your spouse comes home from a medical checkup with fearful news: there are signs that a vicious melanoma has taken hold. The hospital runs emergency tests during the next few days and the news comes back all bad: the prognosis is three months' survival at best, and all that modern medicine can do is mitigate the pain.

I do not want to minimize the staggering blow such news can administer to any family. There are many forms of practical comfort and support that thoughtful people can show. But it must be said that if you are a Christian who has thought about these things in advance, you will recognize that this sentence of death is no different in kind from what you and your spouse have lived under all your life;

that you have been preparing for this day since your conversion; that you have already laid up treasure in heaven, and your heart is there. We are all under sentence of death; we are all terminal cases. The only additional factor is that in this case the sentence, barring a miracle, will certainly be carried out sooner than you had anticipated. I am not pretending that this bare truth is immensely comforting. Our comfort turns on other factors. But full acceptance of this truth can remove a fair bit of unnecessary shock and rebellion; for we will have escaped the modern Western mind-set that refuses to look at death, to plan for death, to live in the light of death, to expect death.

For the believer, the time of death becomes far less daunting a factor when seen in the light of eternity. Although death remains an enemy, an outrage, a sign of judgment, a reminder of sin, and a formidable opponent, it is, from another perspective, the portal through which we pass to consummated life. We pass through death, and death dies. And the more a Christian lives in the consciousness of God's presence here, the easier it is to anticipate the unqualified delight that will be experienced in God's presence there.

Donald A. Carson is Research Professor of New Testament at Trinity Evangelical Divinity School.

Part Three

GOD'S PROVISION IN SUFFERING

18

Just What You Need, Just in Time

CORRIE TEN BOOM

If you are insulted for the name of Christ,
you are blessed, because the Spirit of glory and of God
rests upon you. *1 Peter 4:14*

Several years ago I was in Africa in a little country where an enemy had taken over the government. There was great oppression against the Christians by the new government. The first night I was there some of the native Christians were commanded to come to the police station to be registered. When they arrived they were arrested and during the night they were secretly executed. The next day the same thing happened with other Christians. The third day it was the same. By that time the entire district realized that the Christians were being systematically murdered. It was the intent of the new government to eradicate them all—men, women, and children—much as Hitler tried to eradicate all the Jews.

I was to speak in a little church on Sunday morning. The people came, but I could see fear and tension written on every face. All during the service they looked at each other, their eyes asking the same questions: "Will this one I am sitting beside be the next one to be killed? Will I be the next one?"

I looked out on that congregation of black and white faces. The room was hot and stuffy. Moths and other insects came through the screenless windows and swirled around the naked lightbulbs hanging over the bare, wooden benches upon which the natives sat. They were all looking at me, expecting, hoping, that I could bring them a word from God for this tragic hour. I opened my Bible and read 1 Peter 4:12–14 (PHILLIPS):

> And now, dear friends of mine, I beg you not to be unduly alarmed at the fiery ordeals which come to test your faith, as though this were some abnormal experience. You should be glad, because it means you are called to share Christ's sufferings. One day, when he shows himself in full splendor to men, you will be filled with the most tremendous joy. If you are reproached for being Christ's followers, that is a great privilege, for you can be sure that God's Spirit of glory is resting upon you.

I closed the Book and began to talk simply, as an aunt would talk to her nieces and nephews. "When I was a little girl," I said, "I went to my father and said, 'Daddy, I am afraid that I will never be strong enough to be a martyr for Jesus Christ.'

"'Tell me,' Father said, 'when you take a train trip from Haarlem to Amsterdam, when do I give you the money for the ticket? Three weeks before?'

"'No, Daddy, you give me the money for the ticket just before we get on the train.'

"'That is right,' my father said, 'and so it is with God's strength. Our wise Father in heaven knows when you are going to need things too. Today you do not need the strength to be a martyr; but as soon as you are called upon for the honor of facing death for Jesus, he will supply the strength you need—just in time.'"

I looked out at my African friends. Many of them had already lost loved ones to the firing squad or the headsman's axe. I knew that others would surely die that week. They were listening intently.

"I took great comfort in my father's advice," I said. "Later I had to suffer for Jesus in a concentration camp. He indeed gave me all the courage and power I needed."

My African friends were nodding seriously. They too, believed God would supply all their needs, even the power to face death bravely.

"As soon as you are called upon for the honor of facing death for Jesus, he will supply the strength you need –just in time."

"Tell us more, Tante Corrie," one grizzled old black man said. It was as though they were storing up all the truth they could so they could draw on it in the day of trial.

I told them of an incident that had taken place in the concentration camp at Ravensbruk. "A group of my fellow prisoners had approached me, asking me to tell them some Bible stories. In the concentration camp the guards called the Bible *das Lügenbuch*—the book of lies. Cruel death punishment had been promised for any prisoner who was found possessing a Bible or talking about the Lord. However, I went to my little cot, found my Bible, and retuned to the group of prisoners.

"Suddenly I was aware of a figure behind me. One of the prisoners formed the words with her lips, 'Hide your Bible. It's Lony.' I knew Lony well. She was one of the most cruel of all the *Aufseheriene*—the women guards. However, I knew that I had to obey God who had guided me so clearly to bring a Bible message to the prisoners that morning. Lony remained motionless behind me while I finished my teaching and then I said, 'Let's now sing a hymn of praise.'

"I could see the worried, anxious looks on the faces of the prisoners. Before it had been only me speaking. Now they, too, were going to have to use their mouths to sing. But I felt God wanted us to be bold, even in the face of the enemy. So—we sang.

"When the hymn was finished I heard a voice behind me. 'Another song like that one,' she said. It was Lony. She had enjoyed the singing and wanted to hear more. The prisoners took heart and we sang again—and again. Afterwards I went to her and spoke to her about the Lord Jesus Christ. Strangely, her behavior began to change until, in a crude sort of way, she became a friend."

I finished my story and stood silently while the words took their effect on my African friends. "Let me tell you what I learned from that experience," I told them. "I knew that every word I said could mean death. Yet never before had I felt such peace and joy in my heart as while I was giving the Bible message in the presence of mine enemy. God gave me the grace and power I needed—the money for the train ticket arrived just the moment I was to step on the train."

The faces before me broke into broad grins. Gone were the wrinkles of fear and anxiety. Once again their eyes were flashing with joy and their hearts were filled with peace. I closed the service by reading a poem of Amy Carmichael.

> We follow a scarred Captain,
> Should we not have scars?
> Under His faultless orders
> We follow to the wars.
> Lest we forget, Lord, when we meet,
> Show us Thy hands and feet.[1]

The meeting was over and the Africans stood to leave. Then softly in the back of the room, someone began singing an old gospel song.

There's a land that is fairer than day,
And by faith we can see it afar.
For the Father waits over the way,
To prepare us a dwelling place there.
In the sweet by and by, we shall meet on that beautiful shore,
In the sweet by and by, we shall meet on that beautiful shore.[2]

I don't know how many were killed that week, but someone told me that more than half those who had attended that service met a martyr's death—and thus received a martyr's crown. But I know that God's Spirit of glory had been resting upon them.

Excerpted from *Tramp for the Lord* ©1974 by Corrie ten Boom and James Buckingham, published by CLC Publications, Fort Washington, PA. Used by permission.

Cornelia Johanna Arnolda (Corrie) ten Boom (1892–1983) was a Dutch Christian Holocaust survivor who helped many Jews escape the Nazis during World War II. Her autobiography, *The Hiding Place*, was made into a movie of the same name.

19

Dark Valleys

SINCLAIR FERGUSON

The LORD is my shepherd; I shall not want.
He makes me lie down in green pastures.
He leads me beside still waters.
He restores my soul.
He leads me in paths of righteousness
for his name's sake.
Even though I walk through the valley of the shadow of death,
I will fear no evil,
for you are with me;
your rod and your staff,
they comfort me.
You prepare a table before me
in the presence of my enemies;
you anoint my head with oil;
my cup overflows.
Surely goodness and mercy shall follow me
all the days of my life,
and I shall dwell in the house of the LORD
forever. *Psalm 23*

From childhood onward, most of us are afraid of the dark. In the dark we cannot see our way; we no longer feel in control. We have ceased to be captains of our fate, masters of our destiny. We are in the unknown. The last words of the short-story writer O. Henry are said to have been the words of a popular song: "Turn up the lights, I don't want to go home in the dark." Most of us sympathize with him.

David knew what it was like to be in the dark. "Even though I walk through the valley of the shadow of death, I will fear no evil" (Ps. 23:4).

We usually associate these words with the dark valley of mourning. Beyond all doubt they have a special significance then. For most of us that is the darkest valley of all, the one we most dread entering. But David's language is broader in scope. The valley he describes is, literally, one of deep darkness. The encouragement of his testimony is not to be confined only to the valley of death-shade; it speaks to us in every dark experience of life.

I have to confess with some shame that Psalm 23 has been so familiar to me since childhood that in earlier life I tended to think that the only people who "love Psalm 23" are those whose knowledge of Scripture does not extend much beyond it.

In my own case that disenchantment was increased by reading a child's picture-book version of Psalm 23. The cover picture on the edition I had as a child is still fresh in my memory. David is seated on a rock, his shepherd's crook beside him. He is a beautifully complexioned, curly haired, blue-eyed boy. Nearby his perfectly white sheep graze on rich green pastureland set against a clear blue sky, whose perfection is only heightened by wisps of white cloud. All is well with the shepherd boy as he sweetly composes his psalm of praise. This is an ideal world. David lacks nothing.

Almost everything about this portrayal of Psalm 23 is misleading. Once we see that, we may be able to hear what David is really saying.

His is no ideal world, but one full of dark valleys (v. 4) and the presence of sinister enemies (v. 5). Nor is David an innocent abroad in a safe environment. He is marred, spiritually disfigured, and in danger. No inexperienced youngster this, but a man who has struggled through many difficulties to the confident faith he now confesses.

How can we share his confident faith and be as sure as he was that God will be with us in the darkness?

First we must recognize what David is doing in this psalm. Is he using his experience as a shepherd and his knowledge of sheep as a kind of object lesson, or allegory, of the Christian life? Isn't this a pastoral version of *The Pilgrim's Progress*?

In fact, David is doing something different. His starting point is not sheep and shepherding, but God's word in Scripture. He is, in fact, applying a specific passage from his Bible to his own life and saying to us: "Let me tell you how I experienced its truth and power."

David was not the first person to say, "The Lord is my Shepherd." Those words were spoken first by Jacob—Jacob, the twister-become-prince. At the end of his life, Jacob gave his patriarchal blessing to Joseph's sons Ephraim and Manasseh, saying:

> May the God before whom my fathers Abraham and Isaac walked, *the God who has been my Shepherd all my life* to this day, the Angel who delivered me from all harm—may he bless these boys. (Gen. 48:15–16).

Jacob was a man who had walked through dark valleys—morally, spiritually, emotionally, and physically. Brought up in a family where each parent had favored a different son ("Isaac . . . loved Esau, but Rebekah loved Jacob," Gen. 25:28), he had plotted with his mother to cheat his foolish brother of his birthright (Gen. 25:29–34) and deceive his father (Gen. 27).

In a cruel twist he himself had been similarly deceived by his uncle Laban and found himself married to Leah rather than Rachel, whom he loved (Gen. 29:15–30). He had known fear and loneliness; but in his grace God met with him at Jabbok, wrestled with him, and transformed him into a prince (Gen. 32:22–32; cf. Hos. 12:4).

But Jacob was by no means wholly changed. In later life he would imitate the mistakes of his own parent: "Now [Jacob] loved Joseph more than any of his other sons . . . and he made a richly orna-mented robe for him" (Gen. 37:3). The sins of the fathers appeared to be visited on the children. But God graciously "intended it for good" (Gen. 50:20) as the story of Joseph marvelously illustrates.

Jacob had "struggled with God and with men" (Gen. 32:28). But at the end of his life he could look back and rejoice that the Lord had been his Shepherd, pursuing him like a lost sheep, recuing him, healing him, and providing for him.

In Psalm 23, David is simply saying: "I too have shared the expe-riences of Jacob; I too have wandered in the darkness. And what he discovered I have discovered too: 'The Lord is my shepherd, I shall not be in want.' Let me tell you what this means to me."

When John Wesley lay dying, many of his friends came to visit him. Strong Christians as they were, they were anxious to encour-age him with the promises of God. At one point, however, Wesley raised himself in the bed and with special energy said to them: "Yes, all these promises are true. But *best of all, God is with us.*"

That is the key to what David says. He is able to look the worst of all possible situations in the face and say, "Even though . . . I will fear [not] . . . for *you are with me*" (v. 4). He realizes that if the Lord shepherds him through the darkest valley, then in every other valley in life his presence and power will be sufficient to keep hold of him.

The root of all fears is the fear of death. How can we be deliv-ered from that fear and cut off at its source its ability to feed our lesser fears? The answer, according to David, lies in knowing why the Shepherd's presence and his power can free us from our fear: "for *you* are with me: *your rod and your staff,* they comfort me." The shepherd uses the staff in his hand to work with his sheep, directing, retrieving, disciplining them; the rod or cudgel hangs from his belt, ready to defend them when they come under attack. The sheep look to these things to remind themselves that the shepherd will protect them.

He realizes that if the Lord shepherds him through the darkest valley, then in every other valley in life his presence and power will be sufficient to keep hold of him.

David had often experienced the presence of the Lord as his shepherd protecting and saving him. Yet even David's clear view of God cannot compare with the revelation of the Lord as Shepherd, which is ours:

> I am the good shepherd. The good shepherd lays down his life for the sheep. (John 10:11)
> May the God of peace, who through the blood of the eternal covenant brought back from the dead the Lord Jesus, that great Shepherd of the sheep . . . work in us what is pleasing to him, through Jesus Christ, to whom be glory forever and ever. (Heb. 13:20–21)
> For the Lamb at the center of the throne will be their shepherd; he will lead them to springs of living water. And God will wipe away every tear from their eyes. (Rev. 7:17)

New Testament Christians rejoiced in knowing Christ as their shepherd because he died their death, in their place, for their sin. Their shepherd became a sacrificial lamb, accepted by God. He brings peace to our guilty consciences. Moreover, Christ has been raised. He has conquered death. In him there is resurrection and life, which he shares with all his flock (John 10:10).

David glimpsed this only in outline. We see it all clearly, and our confidence in the Shepherd is all the greater.

We still must face death, as the last enemy. When we think about that we may tremble. But then we remember: Christ has conquered death; it may touch us, but it cannot hold on to us. Even though we walk through death's haunted valley we will fear no evil for Christ is with us.

I was brought up in a small family with my father, mother, and elder brother, and they have all died. My brother died late one night without warning. I remember lying in bed hours later, so overwhelmed by the shock that I wondered whether I could sustain it sufficiently to be able to visit my mother early the next morning to break her heart with the news.

That sad journey, the words that passed between my mother and myself as we clung to each other in the valley of the shadow of death—these are the unforgettable secrets of the soul. But there is something else I cannot forget about those hours, something that sustained me then and has often done so in other circumstances since. As I lay awake, waiting for the dawn and the hour of the dreaded visit as a messenger of sorrow, some words of Scripture, lodged for many years in my memory, seemed to grow from a seed into a mighty tree under whose branches I found shelter from the storm, comfort in my sorrow, light in my darkness.

I felt those words to be true as surely as if I had heard the voice of God speak them from heaven. Here they are:

What then, shall we say in response to this? If God is for us, who can be against us? He who did not spare his own Son, but gave him up for us all—how will he not also, along with him, graciously give us all things?

For I am convinced that neither death . . . neither the present nor the future . . . will be able to separate us from the love of God that is in Christ Jesus our Lord. (Rom. 8:31–32, 38–39)

I cannot imagine living the Christian life on any other basis than this. If the Father loves me so much that he did not spare his own Son but delivered him up to be crucified for me, no further guarantee is needed of his wholehearted and permanent commitment to me and to my blessing.

Whatever happens to me must be seen in that light. Yes, my deepest fears may become realities. I may not be able to understand what God is doing in or to my life; he may seem to be hiding his face from me; my heart may be broken. But can I not trust the One who demonstrated his love for me? When I was helpless in my sin he sent Christ to die for me (Rom. 5:8). If he has done that, will he not work all things together for my good? Will he withhold any thing that is ultimately for the good of those who trust him?

In this way, Christ's death becomes the rod, the cudgel that breaks the necks of the fears that are the enemies of my peace; his word becomes the staff by which he holds on to me and rescues me from danger.

Christ's death becomes the rod,
the cudgel that breaks the necks of the fears
that are the enemies of my peace.

The presence of Christ with me in the valley of deepest darkness is the guarantee that he will always be with me. David reasons thus: he was with me in the valley; therefore "I will dwell in the house of the LORD forever" (v. 6), Having taken us into his flock, the Shepherd gives his word that he will *never* leave us and *never* forsake us (Heb. 13:5). Never means *not now, not ever.*

David realized that this means the Lord would be with him at every stage of his life, in every situation; there and then, in glory, certainly; but also here and now. His "goodness and love" (v. 6) will follow us throughout our lives; dwelling in his house will simply mean more of what we have already begun to experience.

The first physician to die of the AIDS virus in the United Kingdom was a young Christian. He had contracted it while doing medical research in Bulawayo, Zimbabwe. In the last days of his life his powers of communication failed. He struggled with increasing difficulty to express his thoughts to his wife. On one occasion she simply could not understand his message. He wrote on a note pad the letter *J.* She ran through her mental dictionary, saying various words beginning with *J.* None was right. Then she said, "Jesus?"

That was the right word. He was with them. That was all either of them needed to know. That is always enough.

Excerpted from *Deserted by God?* © 1993 by Sinclair B. Ferguson, Banner of Truth Trust, Edinburgh. All rights reserved. Used by permission.

Sinclair Ferguson is a Scottish theologian and senior minister of the First Presbyterian Church in Columbia, South Carolina.

Scripture references are from *The Holy Bible: New International Version.*®

20

Hoped-for Healing

J. I. PACKER

So to keep me from becoming conceited because of the surpassing greatness of the revelations, a thorn was given me in the flesh, a messenger of Satan to harass me, to keep me from becoming conceited. Three times I pleaded with the Lord about this, that it should leave me. But he said to me, "My grace is sufficient for you, for my power is made perfect in weakness." Therefore I will boast all the more gladly of my weaknesses, so that the power of Christ may rest upon me. For the sake of Christ, then, I am content with weaknesses, insults, hardships, persecutions, and calamities. For when I am weak, then I am strong. *2 Corinthians 12:7–10*

It is no wonder that Christians nowadays are so interested in divine healing. They long for the touch of God, as direct and powerful as possible, on their lives (and so they should). They are preoccupied with physical health, to which they feel they have a right. With these concerns dominating their minds, it is not surprising that today many claim that all sick believers may find physical healing through faith, whether through doctors or apart from them. A cynic would say the wish has been father to the thought.

So does Jesus still heal miraculously? Yes, I think that on occasion he does. I do not deny healing miracles today. However, what often is claimed is that healing through prayer, plus perhaps the ministrations of someone with a healing gift, is always available for sick believers, and that if Christian invalids fail to find it, something is lacking in their faith.

It is here that I demur. The reasoning is wrong—cruelly and destructively wrong—as anyone who has sought miraculous healing on this basis and failed to find it or who has had to pick up the pieces in the lives of others who have had that kind of experience knows all too well. To be told that longed-for healing was denied because of some defect in your faith when you had labored and strained every way you knew to devote yourself to God and to "believe for blessing" is to be pitch-forked into distress, despair, and a sense of being abandoned by God.

It is true that Christ's power is still what it was. However, the healings he performed when he was on earth had a special significance. Besides being works of mercy, they were signs of his messianic identity. Jesus' miracles are decisive evidence for all time of who he is and what power he has.

What God has promised and when
he will give it are separate questions.

But supernatural healings in equal abundance to those worked in the days of Jesus' flesh may not be his will today. The question concerns not his power but his purpose. We cannot guarantee that because he healed the sick brought to him then, he will do the same now.

It is true that salvation embraces both body and soul. And there is indeed, as some put it, healing for the body in the atonement. But perfect physical health is not promised for this life. It is promised for heaven as part of the resurrection glory that awaits us in the day when Christ "will change our lowly body to be like his glorious body, by the power that enables him even to subject all things to himself." Full physical well-being is presented as a future blessing of salvation rather than a present one. What God has promised and when he will give it are separate questions.

Further, it is true that blessing is missed where faith is lacking. But even in New Testament times, among leaders who cannot be accused of lacking faith, healing was not universal. We know from Acts that the apostle Paul was sometimes Christ's agent in miraculous healing, and he was himself once miraculously healed of snakebite. Yet he advises Timothy to "use a little wine for the sake of your stomach and your frequent ailments" (1 Tim. 5:23) and informs him that he left Trophimus "ill at Miletus" (2 Tim. 4:20). He also tells the Philippians that their messenger Epaphroditus was so sick that he "nearly died for the work of Christ" and we see how grieved Paul himself had been at the prospect of losing him (Phil. 2:25–27). Plainly, had Paul or anyone else sought power to heal these cases miraculously, he would have been disappointed.

Moreover, Paul himself lived with "a thorn in the flesh" that went unhealed. In 2 Corinthians 12:7–9, he tells us that in three solemn seasons of prayer he had asked Christ, the Lord and the Healer, to take it from him. But the hoped-for healing did not occur. The passage merits close attention.

"Thorn" pictures a source of pain, and "flesh" locates it in Paul's physical or psychological system, thus ruling out the idea, suggested by some, that he might be referring to a difficult colleague. But beyond this, Paul is unspecific, probably deliberately. Guesses about his thorn range from recurring painful illnesses, such as inflamed eyes (see Gal. 4:13–15), migraine, or malaria, to chronic temptation. The former view seems more natural, but nobody can be sure. All we can say is that it was a distressing disability from which Paul could have been delivered on the spot, had Christ so willed.

So Paul lived with pain. The thorn, given him under God's providence, operated as "a messenger of Satan, to harass me" (2 Cor. 12:7) because it tempted him to think hard thoughts about the God who let him suffer, and in resentment to cut back his ministry. How could he be expected to go on traveling, preaching, working day and night, praying, caring, weeping over folk with this pain constantly dragging him down? Such thoughts were "flaming darts of the evil one" (Eph. 6:16) with which he had to contend constantly as the thorn remained unhealed.

Some Christians today live with epilepsy, homosexual cravings, ulcers, and cyclical depressions that plunge them into deep waters of this kind. Philip Hughes is surely correct when, commenting on this passage, he writes: "Is there a single servant of Christ who cannot point to some 'thorn in the flesh,' visible or private, physical or psychological, from which he has prayed to be released, but that has been given him by God to keep him humble, and therefore fruitful? . . . Paul's 'thorn in the flesh' is, by its very lack of definition, a type of every Christian's 'thorn in the flesh.'"

Paul perceived, however, that the thorn was given him not for punishment but for protection. Physical weakness guarded him against spiritual sickness. The worst diseases are those of the spirit—pride, conceit, arrogance, bitterness, self-seeking. They are far more damaging than physical malfunctioning. In 2 Corinthians 12 Paul described the thorn as a sort of prophylactic against pride when he said it was "to keep me from being too elated by the abundance of revelations" (v. 7). He could accept it as a wise provision on the part of his Lord. It was not for want of prayer that the thorn went unhealed. Paul explained to the Corinthians what Christ's response was as he prayed about it. "He said to me, 'My grace is sufficient for you, for my power is made perfect in weakness'" (v. 9). It was as if the Savior was saying, "I can demonstrate my power better by not eliminating your problem. It is better for you, Paul, and for my glory in your life, that I show my strength by keeping you going though the thorn remains."

So Paul embraced his continuing disability as a kind of privilege. "I will all the more gladly boast of my weaknesses, that the power of Christ may rest upon me" (v. 9). The Corinthians, in typical Greek fashion, despised him as a weakling. They did not consider him an elegant speaker or an impressive personality. Paul went even further, telling them that he was weaker than they thought, for he lived with his thorn in the flesh. But Paul learned to glory in his weakness, "for when I am weak, then I am strong" (v. 10). And he wanted the Corinthians to learn to praise God for his weakness, too!

One virtuous commentary doubts whether the thorn could be illness in view of Paul's "extraordinary stamina" throughout his ministry. How obtuse! Extraordinary stamina was precisely what Paul was promised. Similarly obtuse was the reviewer who described Joni Eareckson Tada's books as a testimony to "human courage." Courage, yes—but very much more than human! The age of miraculous blessing is not past, thank God, though such blessing does not always take the form of healing. But then neither did it do so in Paul's day.

Three conclusions issue from what we have seen.

The first concerns miraculous healing. Christ and the apostles only healed miraculously when they were specifically prompted to do so—when, in other words, they knew that to do so was the Father's will. That is why their attempts at healing succeeded. Still, miraculous healing for Christians was not universal then, so there is no warrant for maintaining that it should be so now.

The second conclusion concerns sanctifying providence. God uses chronic pain and weakness, along with other afflictions, as his chisel for sculpting our lives. Felt weakness deepens dependence on

Christ for strength each day. The weaker we feel, the harder we lean. And the harder we lean, the stronger we grow spiritually, even while our bodies waste away. To live with your "thorn" uncomplainingly, sweet, patient, and free in heart to love and help others, even though every day you feel weak, is true sanctification. It is true healing for the spirit. It is a supreme victory of grace. The healing of your sinful person thus goes forward even though the healing of your mortal body does not. And the healing of persons is the name of the game so far as God is concerned.

God uses chronic pain and weakness,
along with other afflictions,
as his chisel for sculpting our lives.

The third conclusion concerns behavior when ill. We should certainly go to the doctor, use medication, and thank God for both. But it is equally certain that we should go to the Lord (Doctor Jesus, as some call him) and ask what challenge, rebuke, or encouragement he might have for us regarding our sickness. Maybe we shall receive healing in the form in which Paul asked for it. Maybe, however, we shall receive it in the form in which Paul received it. We have to be open to both.

Excerpted from *God's Plans for You* © 2001, by J. I. Packer, published by Crossway Books.

James Innell Packer serves as the Board of Governors' Professor of Theology at Regent College in Vancouver, British Columbia.

Scripture references are from *The Revised Standard Version*.

21

Happy in Affliction

THOMAS MANTON

Blessed is the man who remains steadfast under trial, for when he has stood the test he will receive the crown of life, which God has promised to those who love him. *James 1:12*

A Christian is a bird that can sing in winter as well as in spring; he can live in the fire like Moses' bush—burn and not be consumed, even leap in the fire. His joy is from the happy consequences of his sufferings.

"It has been granted to you . . . to suffer for him" (Phil. 1:29). To be called to such special service is an act of God's special favor. Far from being a matter of discouragement, it is a ground for thanksgiving: "If you suffer as a Christian . . . praise God" (1 Pet. 4:16). Do not accuse God with murmuring thoughts but glorify him. This influenced the first saints and martyrs. It is said that they went away "rejoicing because they had been counted worthy of suffering disgrace for the Name" (Acts 5:41); the Greek means that they were honored to be dishonored for Christ.

God has consolations for martyrs, and for his children under trials. Sometimes it is a greater presence of the Word. The sun shines many times when it rains. And they have sweet glimpses of God's favor when their outward condition is most gloomy and sad. Martyrs, in the act of suffering and troubles, not only have sight of their interest, but a sight of the glory of their interest. There are some thoughts stirred up in them that come close to ecstasy; a happy preview makes them almost insensible of their trials and sufferings. They rejoice because they pass into glory more swiftly. The enemies do them a favor by removing them from a troublesome world. This made the early Christians rejoice more when they were condemned than when they were absolved. They kissed the stake and thanked the executioner because of their earnest desires to be with Christ.

But some will say, "My sufferings are not like martyrdom; they do not come from the hand of men, but from providence, and result from my own sins."

It is true there is a difference between afflictions from the hand of God and persecutions from the violence of men. God's hand is just, and guilt will make the soul less cheerful. But remember the apostle's word is "trials of many kinds" and sickness, death of friends, and such things that come from providence are also trials to God's children. These afflictions require not only mourning and humbling, but a holy courage and confidence.

Faith should be above everything that happens to us; it is its work to make a believer triumph over every temporary setback. In ordinary crosses there are many reasons for laughing and joy—such as Christ's companionship; if you do not suffer for Christ, Christ suffers in you, and with you. He is afflicted and touched with a sense of your afflictions. It is wrong for believers to think that Christ is altogether unconcerned by their sorrows unless they are endured for his name's sake, and that the comforts of the gospel are only applicable to martyrdom.

All evils are the same to faith. You should walk so that the world may know you can live above every condition, and that all evils are much beneath your hopes. So, from all that has been said, we see that we should suffer the will of Christ with the same cheerfulness as we should suffer for the name of Christ.

Afflictions do not make the people of God miserable. There is a great deal of difference between a Christian and a man of the world. The latter's best state is vanity (see Ps. 39:5); and a Christian's worst state is happiness. He who loves God is like a die; throw him high or low, he still lands on a solid square. Sometimes he may be afflicted, but he is always happy. There is a double reason for this:

First, outward misery cannot diminish his happiness. A man is never miserable until he has lost his happiness. Our comfort lies to a great extent in the choice of our main happiness. Those who say in effect, "Happy are the people who are in such a case" (see Ps. 144:12–15)—that is, where there is no complaining in their streets, sheep bringing forth thousands, barns full, oxen strong for labor, etc.—may soon be miserable. All these things may disappear at a change of providence, just as Job lost everything in an instant. But those who say, "Blessed [happy] is the people whose God is the Lord"—that is, who count enjoying God as their happiness—when they lose everything, they can still be happy because they have not lost God. Our afflictions reveal our state of mind; when we see outward crosses as the greatest evil, God is not our main happiness. In the greatest lack of earthly things there is happiness, and comfort enough in God's covenant.

Our comfort lies to a great extent in the choice of our main happiness.

Secondly, sometimes as afflictions increase, they bring more comfort and a further experience of grace. God seldom afflicts for no reason. Such dispensations leave us either better or worse. The children of God profit from them, for God recompenses outward losses with inner enjoyments: "For just as the sufferings of Christ flow over into our lives, so also through Christ our comfort overflows" (2 Cor. 1:5). That is, inner comforts can increase with outward sufferings. Learn, then, that people may be happy whom men count miserable. The world judges according to outward appearances and therefore is often mistaken.

There is a comfort in corrections when the discipline is from the Lord: "Blessed is the man you discipline, O LORD, the man you teach from your law" (Ps. 94:12). Corrections aim at the mortifying of sin, and so are more humbling; but trials aim at the discovery of grace, and so are more comfortable. Corrections imply guilt; either we have sinned or are likely to sin, and then God takes up the rod.

We derive no profit at all from affliction—neither grace nor glory—until there is wrestling and exercise. For the sake of grace, the apostle teaches clearly, "Discipline . . . produces a harvest of righteousness and peace for those who have been trained by it" (Heb. 12:11). Trials do not earn us heaven, but they always precede it. Before we are brought to glory, God will first wean us from sin and the world.

"We also rejoice in our sufferings, because we know that suffering produces perseverance" (Rom. 5:3). This rule holds good in all kinds of tribulations or suffering; they bring sweet discoveries of God, and so are matters for joy. They are happy occasions to discover more of God. They give us a greater sense and feeling of the power of grace, and so we may take pleasure in them.

Adapted from the Crossway Classic Commentary *James* by Thomas Manton © 1995 by Watermark, published by Crossway Books.

Thomas Manton (1620–1677) was a Puritan minister who was a clerk at the Westminster Assembly and was known as the "king of preachers." He continued to preach and write even when imprisoned for refusing to cooperate with the Church of England.

Scripture references are from *The Holy Bible: New International Version.*®

22

Power in Weakness

JOHN PIPER

Recently we sang a chorus that goes like this:

Since Jesus came into my heart,
Since Jesus came into my heart,
Floods of joy o'er my soul
Like the sea billows roll
Since Jesus came into my heart.[1]

As we sang it, I wondered how everyone in the chapel was processing that statement in the light of real life experience when sea billows of joy do not roll over the soul. Here's how I fit it in my own experience: Yes, since knowing Jesus, joy has rolled over me like the waves of the sea, but not always. There are times when the tide goes out. God is still God; joy is still joy; but I am baking in the seaweed on the beach waiting for the tide to come in.

What makes days and months and years like that livable is the grace and power of Jesus described in 2 Corinthians 12:1–10 where Paul wrote:

I must boast; there is nothing to be gained by it, but I will go on to visions and revelations of the Lord. I know a man in Christ who fourteen years ago was caught up to the third heaven—whether in the body or out of the body I do not know, God knows. And I know that this man was caught up into Paradise—whether in the body or out of the body I do not know, God knows—and he heard things that cannot be told, which man may not utter. On behalf of this man I will boast, but on my own behalf I will not boast, except of my weaknesses. Though if I wish to boast, I shall not be a fool, for I shall be speaking the truth. But I refrain from it, so that no one may think more of me than he sees in me or hears from me. And to keep me from being too elated by the abundance of revelations, a thorn was given me in the flesh, a messenger of Satan, to harass me, to keep me from being too elated. Three times I besought the Lord about this, that it should leave me; but he said to me, "My grace is sufficient for you, for my power is made perfect in weakness." I will all the more gladly boast of my weaknesses, that the power of Christ may rest upon me. For the sake of Christ, then, I am content with weaknesses, insults, hardships, persecutions, and calamities; for when I am weak, then I am strong.

What are the weaknesses Paul has in mind here when he quotes Jesus as saying in verse 9, "My power is made perfect in weakness"? And then says, "I will all the more gladly boast of my weaknesses"? And then again in verse 10 says, "For the sake of Christ, then, I am content with weaknesses"?

I think the safest way to answer is to let the four other words in verse 10 fill out what he has in mind. What he summarizes as weaknesses in verse 9 he spells out in four other words in verse 10: insults, hardships, persecutions, and calamities.

Insults—when people think of clever ways of making your faith or your lifestyle or your words look stupid or weird or inconsistent.

Hardships—circumstances forced upon you, reversals of fortune against your will. This could refer to any situation where you feel trapped. You didn't plan it or think it would be this way. But there you are, and it's hard.

Persecutions—wounds or abuses or painful circumstances or acts of prejudice or exploitation from people because of your Christian faith or your Christian moral commitments. It's when you are not treated fairly. You get a raw deal.

Calamities (or distresses or difficulties or troubles)—the idea is one of pressure or crushing or being weighed down; circumstances that tend to overcome you with stress and tension.

So you can see that what Paul has in mind here is not sin. He is not talking about a kind of behavior—like we might say he has a weakness for lust; or she has a weakness for overeating. Paul is not talking about bad choices that we make. He is not saying, "The power of Christ is perfected in my bad choices." Or: "I will all the more gladly boast of my bad choices." Weaknesses here are not imperfect behaviors.

They are circumstances and situations and experiences and wounds that make us look weak; things we would probably get rid of if we had the human strength.

If we were "strong," we might return the insult with such an effective put-down that the opponent would wither and everyone would admire our wit and cleverness.

If we were "strong," we might take charge of our own fortune and turn back the emerging hardship and change circumstances so that they go the way we want them to and not force us into discomfort.

If we were "strong," we might turn back the persecution so quickly and so decisively that no one would mess with us again.

If we were "strong," we might use our resources to get out of the calamity or distress as fast as possible, or take charge of the situation and marshal our own resources so masterfully as to minimize its pressure.

But in reality we don't usually have that kind of human strength, and even when we may have it, Christians don't use it the way the world does. Jesus tells us not to return evil for evil (Matt. 5:38–42). Paul said in 1 Corinthians 4:12–13, "When reviled, we bless; when persecuted, we endure; when slandered, we try to conciliate." And then he added, "We have become like the refuse of the world, the off-scouring of all things." In other words, this kind of lifestyle, this kind of response to abuse, looks weak and beggarly and feeble and anemic and inept—at least it looks that way to those who thrive on pride and equate power with the best comeback.

So the answer to our first question is that weaknesses are not sins but rather experiences and situations and circumstances and wounds that are hard to bear and that we can't remove either because they are beyond our control, or because love dictates that we not return evil for evil.

What is the source of such weaknesses? Do they come from Satan or from God? Or both?

Let's take Paul's thorn in the flesh as an example and see what his answer is. In verses 1–4 Paul describes what amazing revelations of God's glory he had been given—he was caught up into Paradise and heard things that cannot be told on earth (vv. 3–4).

How easy it would have been for Paul to think that he was already rising above the ordinary hardships and troubles of earthly life because he was given such a privilege. But verse 7 shows what actually happened: "To keep me from being too elated [RSV; a better translation would be: "to keep me from exalting myself," NASB, or: "to keep me from becoming conceited," NIV] by the abundance of revelations, a thorn was given me in the flesh, a messenger of Satan, to harass me, to keep me from exalting myself."

Now this thorn in the flesh (whether it was some physical problem or some relentless enemies) is one of the weaknesses he is talking about. We know this because when he prays that God would take it away in verse 8 ("three times I besought the Lord"), the Lord answers in verse 9, "My power is made perfect in weakness." So the thorn in the flesh is one of the weaknesses we are talking about.

And where did it come from? Paul calls it a "messenger of Satan"

(v. 7) given to harass him. So one clear answer is that some weaknesses come from Satan. Satan afflicts the children of God through his angels or messengers. His aim is destruction and death and misery.

But it is not that simple, is it? Satan is not the only one at work here. God is at work. This thorn is not just the work of Satan to destroy. It is the work of God to save.

We know this for two reasons. First, because Paul describes the purpose for the thorn in terms of preventing pride. But Satan's whole design is to produce pride not prevent it. That's how he kills: either with pride in what we have done, or despair over what we haven't done. Paul's revelations in Paradise made him vulnerable to pride and self-exaltation. So God uses the hostile intentions of Satan for Paul's holiness. Satan wanted to make Paul miserable and turn him away from the faith and the ministry and the value of the visions he had seen. But God wanted to make Paul humble and turn him away from self-exaltation. So God appointed the thorn of Satan for the work of salvation.

This thorn is not just the work of Satan
to destroy. It is the work of God to save.

The other reason we know the thorn is God's work and not just Satan's is that when Paul prays in verse 8 that God would take the thorn away, the Lord says, No, because my power is made perfect in this weakness. In other words, I have a purpose in what is happening to you. This is not ultimately Satan's destroying work. It is ultimately my saving, sanctifying work.

Just like it was with Job—God permits Satan to afflict his righteous servant, and turns the affliction for his good purposes. (See also Luke 22:31–32.)

So the answer to our second question is that the source of our weaknesses may sometimes be Satan and his destructive designs for us; but always our weaknesses are designed by God for our good. This is why the truth of God's sovereign grace is so precious in the midst of hardship and calamity. God is in control of Satan. Satan does nothing to God's children that God does not design with infinite skill and love for our good.

Which brings us to the final question, which we have already answered.

What is the purpose of such weaknesses? Is there a goal or an aim for why the weaknesses come? Why insults, hardships, persecutions, calamities, troubles? Why can't I find a job? Why am I trapped in this awful marriage? Why does my dad have cancer? Why can't I have children? Why do I have no friends? Why is nothing working in my life?

Paul gives three brief answers about his own experience and I think they are tremendously important for us to live by.

First, he says that Satan has the purpose to buffet you or harass you (v. 7). And so it is okay to pray for relief. That's what Paul did until he got word from the Lord. Pain is not a good thing in itself. God does not delight in your suffering. Satan does and he must be resisted.

Second, God's purpose over and through Satan's harassment is our humility. Paul was in danger of pride and self-exaltation and God took steps to keep him humble. This is an utterly strange thing in our self-saturated age. God thinks humility is more important than comfort. Humility is more important than freedom from pain. He will give us a mountain-top experience in Paradise, and then bring us through anguish of soul lest we think that we have risen above the need for total reliance on his grace. So his purpose is our humility and lowliness and reliance on him (cf. 2 Cor. 1:9; 4:7).

Finally, God's purpose in our weaknesses is to glorify the grace and power of his Son. This is the main point of verses 9–10. Jesus says, "My grace is sufficient for you, for my power is made perfect in weakness." God's design is to make you a showcase for Jesus' power. But not necessarily the way the market demands: not by getting rid of all our weaknesses; but by giving strength to endure and even rejoice in tribulation.

Let God be God here. If he wills to show the perfection of his Son's power in our weakness instead of by our escape from weakness, then he knows best; trust him. Hebrews 11 is a good guide here. It says that by faith some escaped the edge of the sword (v. 34) and by faith some were killed by the sword (v. 37). By faith some stopped the mouths of lions, and by faith others were sawn asunder. By faith some were mighty in war, and by faith others suffered chains and imprisonment (see also Phil. 4:11–13).

The deepest need that you and I have in weakness and adversity is not quick relief, but the well-grounded confidence that what is happening to us is part of the greatest purpose of God in the universe.

The ultimate purpose of God in our weakness is to glorify the kind of power that moved Christ to the cross and kept him there until the work of love was done. Paul said that Christ crucified was foolishness to the Greeks, a stumbling block to the Jews, but to those who are called it is the power of God and the wisdom of God (1 Cor. 1:23f.).

The deepest need that you and I have in weakness and adversity is not quick relief, but the well-grounded confidence that what is happening to us is part of the greatest purpose of God in the universe—the glorification of the grace and power of his Son—the grace and power that bore him to the cross and kept him there until the work of love was done. That's what God is building into our lives. That is the meaning of weakness, insults, hardships, persecution, calamity.

Adapted from the sermon "Christ's Power Is Made Perfect in Weakness" by John Piper, given at Bethlehem Baptist Church, July 14, 1991. This sermon can be found in its entirety at http://www.desiringgod.org/ResourceLibrary/Sermons/ByScripture/20/766_Christs_Power_Is_Made_Perfect_in_Weakness/.

John Piper is pastor for preaching and vision at Bethlehem Baptist Church in Minneapolis, Minnesota.

Scripture references are from *The Revised Standard Version*.

23

To Suffer as Christ Did

MARTIN LUTHER

When he was reviled, he did not revile in return;
when he suffered, he did not threaten,
but continued entrusting himself to him who judges justly.

1 Peter 2:23

Christ has gone before and left you an example of perfect patience under the most intense suffering, an example equaled nowhere in the world. The Supreme Majesty, God's own Son, suffered in the most ignominious manner the extremity of torture, pain, and anguish in body and soul, something intolerable to mere human nature; and that innocently, for us condemned sinners—suffering for the sins of strangers.

"Who, when he was reviled, reviled not again; when he suffered threatened not."

Christ did no sin, neither was guile found in his mouth. Why, then, did the Jews persecute and crucify him—put him to death? Inquire into his entire life history and you will find that no one could justly impeach, nor could convict, him for any sin. He himself appealed to his enemies to prove aught of sin in him. No one could show an injury he had ever done to anyone, or a wrong he had ever taught or practiced. On the contrary, he had gone about to bring to the Jewish nation the grace and salvation of God. He had revealed God's Word, opened the eyes of the blind, healed the sick, cast out devils, fed great multitudes when hungry and lacking food. In short, in all his life, there was nothing in word or act but truth, goodness, beneficence, and a disposition to aid. In return for the good he wrought, he was compelled to receive the ungrateful reward of man's hatred and condemnation. His enemies were moved solely by obdurate, diabolical hatred, and could not cease their persecutions until they brought him to the cross, where he was disgracefully hung up nude between two murderers, being lifted up as unworthy to touch the earth and to live among men.

Christ was under no obligation to endure disgrace and ill-treatment. He might have refrained from his benevolent ministrations when he saw the futility of his efforts with the Jews. But he did not so; even in his sufferings upon the cross he charitably prayed for his enemies. He had authority, he had power enough, and he would have been justified in the action, had he revenged himself on his furious enemies, invoked evil upon them, and execrated them as they deserved to be execrated; for they had treated him with gross injustice before all the world, as even the testimony of his betrayer and his judge and all creatures admitted, and had bitterly reviled him when he hung upon the cross. But he did none of these things. He bore with ineffable meekness and patience all the ill-treatment his enemies could heap upon him. Even in his extremity of anguish, he benevolently interceded for them to his heavenly Father, to which act the prophet Isaiah (ch. 53) offers a tribute of high praise.

Notice, we have here in all respects a perfect and inimitable example of patience—patience of the most exalted kind. In this example we may behold as in a glass what we have yet to learn of calm endurance, and thus be impelled to imitate that example in some small measure at least.

He bore with ineffable meekness and patience all the ill-treatment his enemies could heap upon him.

Not without reason does Peter applaud the fact that when Christ was reviled he reviled not again, and when he suffered he threatened not. Though to endure undeserved violence and injustice is hard enough, that which more than aught else naturally renders suffering grievous and makes men impatient is to experience the monstrous unfairness of receiving the mean and vexatious reward of ingratitude from individuals who have enjoyed one's favors and greatest benefactions. Base ingratitude is extremely painful for human nature to endure. It makes the heart flutter and the blood boil with a spirit of revenge. When no alternative presents, an outburst of reviling, execration, and threatening follows. Flesh and blood has not the power of restraint to enable it to remain calm when evil is returned for favors and benevolence, and to say, "God be thanked."

Mark the example of Christ, however, and there learn to censure yourself. Beloved, how can you complain when you see how infinitely greater was the grief and how much more painful the anxiety endured by your beloved Lord and faithful Savior, the Son of God himself, who yet bore all patiently and submissively and, more than that, prayed for those instrumental in causing that agony? Who with a single drop of Christian blood in his heart would not blush with shame to be guilty of murmuring at his sufferings when, before God, he is so sinful and is deserving of much more affliction? Wicked, unprofitable and condemned servant must he be who does not follow his Lord's example of endurance but presumes to think himself better and nobler than Christ; who with inimical spirit murmurs, complaining of great injustice, when he really deserves affliction, and when he suffers infinitely less than did his dear, righteous, innocent Lord. Beloved, if Christ so suffered in return for the great blessing he conferred, be not too indolent to imitate him in some degree by suffering without anger and reproaches. Less reason have you to be angry and reproachful from the fact that you, too, were one whose sins brought Christ to the cross.

Having fulfilled his official duties, and the hour of his suffering having arrived, Christ suffered patiently, permitting his enemies to heap upon him all possible evil in return for his manifested love and blessings. Instead of angrily reviling and execrating while, suspended from the cross, he endured the most shameful calumnies, he, with strong cries and with tears, prayed, "Father, forgive them." It was, indeed, a heart of unfathomable love that, in the midst of extreme suffering, had compassion on its persecutors and blessed them in greater measure than parent can bless child or one individual bless another.

Assuredly God will not allow himself to be deceived. He will, in due time, relieve the innocent victim of injustice, and his punishment will seek out the wicked.

Peter says, further,

"But committed himself to him that judgeth righteously."

Who revealed to Peter the nature of Christ's thoughts upon the cross? The apostle has just been saying that Christ reviled not nor thought of revenge, but rather manifested love and good will toward his virulent enemies. How could Christ approve such malice? Truly he could not endorse it. Nor could he commend his enemies for crucifying him and putting him to death upon the cross without cause.

No such conclusion may be drawn. The devil and his adherents must not construe the passage to mean license to heap all manner of torture and distress upon Christ and his saints as upon those who must not only patiently bear these things, unmoved by revengeful desires, but must render gratitude to their persecutors as if their acts were praiseworthy. No; this can by no means be permitted. Could I be said to suffer innocently if I am obliged to confess I am well treated? Several times in this epistle Peter admonishes Christians not to suffer as evil-doers, thieves, murderers. But if I suffer innocently and am unjustly treated, I am not to justify the ill-treatment and strengthen the enemy in his sins; for, so doing, I would approve his conduct and assume the guilt attributed.

When Peter made this little statement about Christ not reviling nor threatening, which was true, he did not mean that Christ justified his persecutors in their treatment of him. But what are we to do? If we do not justify our enemies when they make us suffer, they will do even worse things to us; for they desire the name and the credit, in the eyes of the world, of having done right by us. Yes, as Christ has somewhere said, they would have it thought they do God great service by murdering us. Now, who is to judge and decide the question?

Peter declares that Christ committed the matter to him who judges righteously. How should he do otherwise, knowing that his persecutors treated him unjustly and yet maintained the contrary? There was for him no judge on earth. He was compelled to commit the matter to that righteous judge, his heavenly Father. Well he knew that such sins and blasphemies could not go unpunished. No, the sentence was already passed, the sword sharpened, the angels given orders, for the overthrow of Jerusalem. Previous to his sufferings, on his way to Jerusalem, as Christ beheld the city, he announced its coming doom and wept over it. Therefore, he prays for his enemies, saying: "Dear Father, I must commit the matter to thee, since they refuse to hear or to see the wrong they do. Well I know they are rushing into thy wrath and thy terrible punishment, but I pray thee to forgive them what they do to me." And so they would have been forgiven had they afterward repented at the apostles' preaching, and had they not further sinned in persecuting God's Word and thus brought upon their unrepentant selves ultimate punishment.

As Christ did, so should we conduct ourselves in our sufferings; not approving or assenting to whatever may be heaped upon us, but yet not seeking revenge.

Observe, as Christ did, so should we conduct ourselves in our sufferings; not approving or assenting to whatever may be heaped upon us, but yet not seeking revenge. We are to commit the matter to God, who will judge aright. We cannot maintain our rights before the world; therefore we must commit our cause to God, who judges righteously and who will not allow calumniation of his Word and persecution of believers to pass unpunished. We must, however, pray for our persecutors, that they may be converted and escape future wrath and punishment; and so we do.

Such, mark you, is the example of Christ, presented to the entire Christian church—set up as a pattern for her. Hence it is the duty of the church, as Peter elsewhere tells us, to arm herself with the same mind which was Christ's, to suffer as Christ did and to think: If Christ, my Lord and Leader, has suffered for me with so great meekness and patience, how much more reason have I to submit to suffering! And what can it harm me to suffer when I know it is God's will? Not because the suffering in itself is so perfecting and precious, but for the sake of the dear Saviour who suffered for me.

A sermon by Martin Luther; taken from his Church Postil, originally published in 1909 in English by The Luther Press (Minneapolis, MN), as *Luther's Epistle Sermons, vol. 2.*

Martin Luther (1483–1546) was a German monk, theologian, and church reformer whose ideas sparked the Protestant Reformation and changed the course of Western civilization.

24

Learning to Be Content

JEREMIAH BURROUGHS

I have learned in whatever situation I am to be content.
I know how to be brought low, and I know how
to abound. In any and every circumstance,
I have learned the secret of facing plenty and hunger,
abundance and need. I can do all things through him
who strengthens me. *Philippians 4:11–13*

To a carnal heart the only way to contentment is the removing of the affliction. O that it may be gone! "No," says a gracious heart, "God has taught me a way to be content though the affliction itself still continues." There is a power of grace to turn this affliction into good; it takes away the sting and poison of it.

Take the case of poverty, a man's possessions are lost: Well, is there no way to be contented till your possessions are made up again? Till your poverty is removed? Yes, certainly, Christianity would teach contentment, though poverty continues. It will teach you how to turn your poverty to spiritual riches. You shall be poor still as to your outward possessions, but this shall be altered; whereas before it was a natural evil to you, it comes now to be turned to a spiritual benefit to you. And so you come to be content.

There is a saying of Ambrose, "Even poverty itself is riches to holy men." Godly men make their poverty turn to riches; they get more riches out of their poverty than ever they get out of their revenues. Out of all their trading in this world they never had such incomes as they have had out of their poverty. This a carnal heart will think strange, that a man shall make poverty the most gainful trade that ever he had in the world. I am persuaded that many Christians have found it so, that they have gotten more good by their poverty than ever they got by all their riches. You find it in Scripture. You do not find one godly man who came out of an affliction worse than when he went into it; though for a while he was shaken, yet at last he was better for an affliction.

But a great many godly men, you find, have been worse for their prosperity. Scarcely one godly man that you read of in Scripture but was worse for prosperity (except for Daniel and Nehemiah—I do not read of any hurt they got by their prosperity); scarcely, I think, is there one example of a godly man who was not worse for his prosperity than better. So you see it is no strange thing to one who is gracious that they shall get good by their affliction.

God has given a Christian such power that
he can turn afflictions into mercies,
darkness into light.

A Christian is partaker of the divine nature, so the Scripture says; grace is part of the divine nature, and, being part of the divine nature, it has an impression of God's omnipotent power, that is, to create light out of darkness, to bring good out of evil—by this way a Christian comes to be content. God has given a Christian such power that he can turn afflictions into mercies, darkness into light.

If a man had the power that Christ had, when the water pots were filled, he could by a word turn the water into wine. If you who have nothing but water to drink had the power to turn it into wine, then you might be contented; certainly a Christian has received this power from God, to work thus miraculously. It is the nature of grace to turn water into wine, that is, to turn the water of your affliction, into the wine of heavenly consolation.

When we say of grace, that it can turn water into wine, and turn poverty into riches, and make poverty a gainful trade, a carnal heart says, "Let them have that trade if they will, and let them have water to drink, and see if they can turn it into wine." Oh, take heed you do not speak in a scornful way of the ways of God; grace has the power to turn afflictions into mercies. Two men may have the same affliction; to one it shall be as gall and wormwood, yet it shall be wine and honey and delightfulness and joy and advantage and riches to the other. This is the mystery of contentment, not so much by removing the evil, as by metamorphosing the evil, by changing the evil into good.

In all the afflictions, all the evils that befall him, a Christian can see love, and can enjoy the sweetness of love in his afflictions as well as in his mercies. The truth is that the afflictions of God's people come from the same eternal love that Jesus Christ came from. Jerome said, "He is a happy man who is beaten when the stroke is a stroke of love." All God's strokes are strokes of love and mercy, all God's ways are mercy and truth, to those that fear him and love him (Ps. 25:10). The ways of God, the ways of affliction, as well as the ways of prosperity, are mercy and love to him.

Grace gives a man an eye to see the love of God in every affliction as well as in prosperity. Now this is a mystery to a carnal heart. They can see no such thing; they think God loves them when he prospers them and makes them rich, but they think God loves them not when he afflicts. Grace enables men to see love in the very frown of God's face, and so comes to receive contentment.

Grace gives a man an eye to see the love of God in every affliction as well as in prosperity.

A godly man has contentment because just as he sees all his afflictions come from the same love that Jesus Christ did, so he sees them all sanctified in Jesus Christ, sanctified in a Mediator. He sees, I say, all the sting and venom and poison of them taken out by the virtue of Jesus Christ, the Mediator between God and man. For instance, when a Christian would have contentment he works it out thus:

What is my affliction? Is it poverty that God strikes me with? Jesus Christ had not a house to hide his head in, the fowls of the air had nests, and the foxes holes, but the Son of man had not a hole to hide his head in; now my poverty is sanctified by Christ's poverty. I can see by faith the curse and sting and venom taken out of my poverty by the poverty of Jesus Christ.

Christ Jesus was poor in this world to deliver me from the curse of my poverty. So my poverty is not afflictive, if I can be contented in such a condition. That is the way, not to stand and repine, because I have not what others have; no, but instead to say, I am poor, and Christ was poor, that he might bless my poverty to me.

Am I disgraced or dishonored? Is my good name taken away? Why, Jesus Christ had dishonor put upon him; he was called Beelzebub, and a Samaritan, and they said he had a devil in him. All the foul aspersions that could be were cast upon Jesus Christ, and this was for me, that I might have the disgrace that is cast upon me sanctified to me.

Others abuse and speak ill of me, but did they not abuse Jesus

Christ, and speak ill of him? And what am I in comparison of Christ? The subjection of Christ to such an evil was for me, that though such a thing should come upon me, I might know that the curse of it is taken from me through Christ's subjection to that evil.

Am I in great bodily pain? Jesus Christ had as great pain in his body as I have.

The exercising of faith on what Christ endured, is the way to get contentment in the midst of our pains.

Have you ever tried this way of getting contentment, to act your faith on all the pains and sufferings that Jesus Christ suffered? A Christian gets contentment when under pains, in this way. Sometimes one who is very godly and gracious may be found bearing grievous pains and extremities very cheerfully, and you wonder at it. He gets it by acting his faith upon what pains Jesus Christ suffered.

You are afraid of death? The way to get contentment is by exercising your faith on the death of Jesus Christ. It may be that you have inward troubles in your soul, and God withdraws himself from you; still your faith is to be exercised upon the sufferings that Jesus Christ endured in his soul. He poured forth his soul before God, and when he sweat drops of water and blood, he was in an agony in his very spirit, and he found even God himself about to forsake him. Now thus to act your faith on Jesus Christ brings contentment, and is not this a mystery to carnal hearts? A gracious heart finds contentment as a mystery; it is no marvel that St. Paul said, "I am instructed in a mystery, to be contented in whatsoever condition I am in."

Adapted from *The Rare Jewel of Christian Contentment* by Jeremiah Burroughs.

Jeremiah Burroughs (1600–1646) was a Puritan preacher and a member of the Westminster Assembly.

25

Refuge and Rest in Christ

JONATHAN EDWARDS

Each will be like a hiding place from the wind,
a shelter from the storm,
like streams of water in a dry place,
like the shade of a great rock in a weary land. *Isaiah 32:2*

There are quiet rest and sweet refreshment in Christ for God's people that are weary. The saints themselves, while they remain in this imperfect state, and have so much remains of sin in their hearts, are liable still to many troubles and sorrows, and much weariness, and have often need to resort anew unto Jesus Christ for rest. I shall mention three cases wherein Christ is a sufficient remedy.

First, there is rest and sweet refreshment in Christ for those that are wearied with persecutions. It has been the lot of God's church in this world for the most part to be persecuted. It has had now and then some lucid intervals of peace and outward prosperity, but generally it has been otherwise. This has accorded with the first prophecy concerning Christ: "I will put enmity between thee and the woman, and between thy seed and her seed." Those two seeds have been at enmity ever since the time of Abel. Satan has borne great malice against the church of God, and so have those that are his seed. And oftentimes God's people have been persecuted to an extreme degree, have been put to the most exquisite torments that wit or art could devise, and thousands of them have been tormented to death.

But even in such a case there are rest and refreshment to be found in Christ Jesus. When their cruel enemies have given them no rest in this world; when, as oftentimes has been the case, they could not flee, nor in any way avoid the rage of their adversaries, but many of them have been tormented gradually from day to day, that their torments might be lengthened; still rest has been found even then in Christ. It has been often found by experience; the martyrs have often showed plainly that the peace and calm of their minds were undisturbed in the midst of the greatest bodily torment, and have sometimes rejoiced and sung praises upon the rack and in the fire. If Christ is pleased to send forth his Spirit to manifest his love, and speaks friendly to the soul, it will support it even in the greatest outward torment that man can inflict. Christ is the joy of the soul, and if the soul be but rejoiced and filled with divine light, such joy no man can take away; whatever outward misery there be, the spirit will sustain it.

Secondly. There is in Christ rest for God's people, when exercised with afflictions. If a person labor under great bodily weakness, or under some disease that causes frequent and strong pains, such things will tire out so feeble a creature as man. It may to such one be a comfort and an effectual support to think that he has a Mediator, who knows by experience what pain is; who by his pain has purchased eternal ease and pleasure for him; and who will make his brief sufferings to work out a far more exceeding delight to be bestowed when he shall rest from his labours and sorrows.

If a person be brought into great straits as to outward subsistence, and poverty brings abundance of difficulties and extremities; yet it may be a supporting, refreshing consideration to such one to think that he has a compassionate Savior, who when upon earth, was so poor that he had nowhere to lay his head, and who became poor to make him rich, and purchased for him durable riches, and will make his poverty work out an exceeding and eternal weight of glory.

If God in his providence calls his people to mourn over lost relations, and if he repeats his stroke and takes away one after another of those that were dear to him; it is a supporting, refreshing consideration to think that Christ has declared that he will be in stead of all relations unto those who trust in him. They are as his mother, and sister, and brother; he has taken them into a very near relation to himself: and in every other afflictive providence, it is a great comfort to a believing soul to think that he has an intercessor with God, that by him he can have access with confidence to the throne of grace, and that in Christ we have so many great and precious promises, that all things shall work together for good, and shall issue in eternal blessedness. God's people, whenever they are scorched by afflictions as by hot sun-beams, may resort to him, who is as a shadow of a great rock, and be effectually sheltered, and sweetly refreshed.

God's people, whenever they are scorched
by afflictions as by hot sun-beams,
may resort to him, who is as a shadow of
a great rock, and be effectually sheltered,
and sweetly refreshed.

Thirdly. There is in Christ quiet rest and sweet refreshment for God's people when wearied with the buffetings of Satan. The devil, that malicious enemy of God and man, does whatever lies in his power to darken and hinder, and tempt God's people, and render their lives uncomfortable. Often he raises needless and groundless scruples, and casts in doubts, and fills the mind with such fear as is tormenting, and tends to hinder them exceedingly in the Christian course; and he often raises mists and clouds of darkness, and stirs up corruption, and thereby fills the mind with concern and anguish, and sometimes wearies out the soul. So that they may say as the psalmist: "Many bulls have compassed me: strong bulls of Bashan have beset me round. They gaped upon me with their mouths, as a ravening and a roaring lion."

In such a case if the soul flies to Jesus Christ, they may find rest in him, for he came into the world to destroy Satan, and to rescue souls out of his hands. And he has all things put under his feet, whether they be things in heaven, or things on earth, or things in hell, and therefore he can restrain Satan when he pleases. And that he is doubtless ready enough to pity us under such temptations, we may be assured, for he has been tempted and buffeted by Satan as well as we. He is able to succour those that are tempted, and he has promised that he will subdue Satan under his people's feet. Let God's people therefore, when they are exercised with any of those kinds of weariness, make their resort unto Jesus Christ for refuge and rest.

Excerpted from the sermon "Safety, Fullness, and Sweet Refreshment in Christ" found in "Seventeen Occasional Sermons" in *The Works of Jonathan Edwards*.

Jonathan Edwards (1703–1758) was a colonial American Congregational preacher, theologian, missionary to native Americans, and president of the College of New Jersey which later became Princeton University.

Scripture quotations are from the *King James Version* of the Bible.

Notes

Chapter 1: Suffering: The Servant of Our Joy

1. Reynolds Price, *Letter to a Man in the Fire: Does God Exist and Does He Care?* (New York: Touchstone, 1999), 64.

2. Fyodor Dostoevsky, *The Brothers Karamazov* (New York: Farrar, Straus and Giroux, 2002), 235–36.

Chapter 2: The Gift of Pain

1. Dorothy Sayers, *The Greatest Drama Ever Staged* (London: Hodder & Stoughton, 1938).

Chapter 4: When We Don't Know Why, We Trust God Who Knows Why

1. Jean Paul Sartre, *The Devil and the Good Lord*, trans. Kitty Black (New York: Vintage Books, 1960), 140–41.

2. Elie Wiesel, *Night* (New York: Avon Books, 1969), 44.

3. C. S. Lewis, *A Grief Observed* (London: Faber & Faber, 1966), 25.

4. Roland H. Bainton, *Here I Stand: A Life of Martin Luther* (New York: Penguin, 1995), 290.

Chapter 8: Bearing Suffering

1. In his Greek New Testament Bonhoeffer underlined the word *auvtou'*, "their [cross]," in Matthew 16:24 and wrote in the margin, "*dei'predest[inatio]!*"—"Must—predestination!"

2. In Matthew 27:46, Jesus on the cross quotes Psalm 22:1: "My God, my God, why have you forsaken me?"

3. Bonhoeffer took this quotation from Witte's *Nun freut euch lieben Christen gemein*, 243–44. Bonhoeffer's copy is marked at this place. Witte, in turn, quoted from Luther's second edition of "The Seven Penitential Psalms," 1525 (*LW* 14:152 [*WA* 18:489, 15–27]).

Chapter 16: Choosing Trust

1. Newton, *The Works of John Newton* (Edinburgh: The Banner of Truth Trust, 1985), vol. 5, 621–22.

2. Newton, *The Works of John Newton*, vol. 5, 622–23.

3. Newton, *The Works of John Newton*, vol. 5, 623–24.

Chapter 18: Just What You Need, Just in Time

1. Amy Carmichael, "Royal Scar" ©1931 The Dohnavur Fellowship, 80 Windmill Rd, Brentford, Middx, TW8 0QH, UK.

2. "Sweet By and By," text by Sanford F. Bennett.

Chapter 22: Power in Weakness

1. Text by Rufus H. McDaniel and music by Charles H Gabriel ©1914, © renewal 1942 by The Rodeheaver Co. (a div. of Word, Inc.).

Scripture Index

Genesis

12:1	66
25:28	129
25:29–34	129
Chap. 27	129
29:15–30	130
32:22–32	130
32:28	130
37:3	130
45:5	50
48:15–16	129
50:19–20	45
50:20	11, 31, 50, 130

Leviticus

26:23–24	52

Deuteronomy

28:1	52

Judges

13:20	91
13:22–23	91

1 Samuel

21:12	109

2 Samuel

10:12	52

Job

Chap. 1	31
1:21	50
42:5	75

Psalms

16:8	109
22:1	171n2
Chap. 23	127–31, 134
23:4	11, 109, 128, 130
23:5	129
25:10	163
34:4	111
39:5	143
39:9	51
56:4	111
56:11	109
Chap. 90	116
90:3–4	113
90:9–12	113
94:12	144
144:12–15	143

Isaiah

32:2	167
45:7	52
49:1–3	85
49:2–3	81

Chap. 53	154	24:13–27	45–46
53:2–4	69		
		John	
Lamentations		9:3	11
3:38	52	10:10	132
		10:11	131
Hosea		12:24	18
12:4	130		
		Acts	
Amos		5:41	141
3:6	52	20:24	72
Habakkuk		**Romans**	
1:2–3	55	5:3	144
2:4	58	5:3–5	18
		5:8	133
Zechariah		8:18	20, 23, 29
13:9	87	8:19	29
		8:22	23, 29
Matthew		8:23	11, 29
5:38–42	147	8:28	11, 33, 43, 47
5:45	99	8:31–32	133
11:30	66	8:38–39	133
16:24	171n1		
26:39	65	**1 Corinthians**	
26:42	65	1:23	151
26:74	63	4:12–13	147
27:46	37, 171n2		
		2 Corinthians	
Mark		1:5	144
8:34	63	1:9	151
		1:20	10
Luke		4:7	151
9:23	33	4:8–12	17
22:31–32	150	4:14	19

4:16–17	15, 20		13:5	134
4:17	35		13:20–21	131
11:24–28	16		**James**	
12:1–10	145–52		1:12	141
12:7–10	135, 137–39			
12:9	11		**1 Peter**	
Galatians			1:6–7	103
4:13–15	137		2:21	33
			2:23	153
Ephesians			4:1	34
1:11–12	49		4:12–14	122
6:12	51		4:14	121
6:16	138		4:16	141
Philippians			**Revelation**	
1:29	141		7:17	131
2:25–27	137			
3:10	33			
4:11–13	151, 161			
Colossians				
3:4	72			
1 Timothy				
5:23	137			
2 Timothy				
4:20	137			
Hebrews				
6:17–19	9–10			
11:34	151			
11:37	151			
12:11	144			